Boxers

CYNTHIA P. GALLAGHER

Boxers

Project Team
Editor: Stephanie Fornino
Copy Editor: Ellen Bingham
Interior Design: Leah Lococo Ltd. and Stephanie Krautheim
Design Layout: Tilly Grassa

T.F.H. Publications
President/CEO: Glen S. Axelrod
Executive Vice President: Mark E. Johnson
Publisher: Christopher T. Reggio
Production Manager: Kathy Bontz

T.F.H. Publications, Inc.
One TFH Plaza
Third and Union Avenues
Neptune City, NJ 07753

Discovery Communications, Inc. Book Development Team
Maureen Smith, Executive Vice President & General Manager, Animal Planet
Carol LeBlanc, Vice President, Marketing and Retail Development
Elizabeth Bakacs, Vice President, Creative Services
Peggy Ang, Director, Animal Planet Marketing
Caitlin Erb, Marketing Associate

Printed and bound in China

06 07 08 09 10 1 3 5 7 9 8 6 4 2

Library of Congress Cataloging-in-Publication Data
Gallagher, Cynthia P.
   Boxers / Cynthia P. Gallagher.
      p. cm. — (Animal Planet pet care library)
   Includes index.
   ISBN 0-7938-3759-6 (alk. paper)
   1. Boxer (Dog breed) I. Animal Planet (Television network) II. Title. III. Series.
   SF429.G63G35 2006
   636.73—dc22

The Leader In Responsible Animal Care For Over 50 Years!™

www.tfhpublications.com

Table of Contents

Chapter 1

Why I Adore My

Boxer

It has been said that the Boxer is the most gifted of canines, with a special talent for worming his way into the good graces and hearts of an entire household.

This sums it up for all of us. The Boxer rules, if not reigns, in popularity. He is among the top ten most commonly registered dog breeds of the American Kennel Club (AKC). His versatility, temperament, and low-maintenance grooming make us wonder why anyone would want any other breed.

S ince the late 1800s, many parts of the world have come to discover the handsome looks and delightful personality embodied in this one canine package.

Origin of the Boxer

The Boxer descends from the Brabanter Bullenbeisser (BB), an ancient hunting and bull-baiting dog originating in the Belgian town of Brabant during the Middle Ages. He became a favorite hunting companion of southern German noblemen. Described in historical accounts as dark-colored, usually a fawn or brindle with a black mask, the BB's undershot jaw—a very short muzzle with the lower jaw extending beyond the upper jaw—facilitated breathing while allowing the dog to keep a bite-hold on a bull or boar. Ears were cropped short to prevent injury, a practical custom that has endured into today's purely cosmetic alteration.

After the Napoleonic Wars dispersed the

In ancient times, the Boxer was a favorite hunting companion of southern German noblemen.

aristocracy, which comprised the majority of BB owners, local butchers and cattle dealers used the breed to drive livestock and physically bite-hold an animal for slaughter. Such work required independent thinking, a trait perpetuated in modern Boxers. The BB attacked prey from behind, grabbing it by the neck or back, much like the training early Boxers received for protection work. By the 19th century, the role of the BBs had shifted from hunting companion of the elite to indispensable dog of the working class.

Popular belief has the early 19th-century BB bred with an early Bulldog, another hunting and working breed. Early Bulldogs were taller than their modern-day counterparts, with a smaller head, and the resulting progeny was the foundation of today's Boxer. Germany continued its fascination with this new breed, although it is not clear why it ended up with an English name. It could be a derivation of *Boxl*, a similar type of 19th-century German dog. A widely held thought is that the dog's unique use of his forelegs in fighting and playing led to the name *Boxer*.

The numerous varieties in breed type at that time made it necessary to define exactly what a Boxer should look like. This definition, called the breed standard, was developed by the first German Boxer club, established in 1895 in Munich. Shortly thereafter, the first Boxer show was held, and conformation breeding began in earnest.

What Does the Boxer Look Like?

The first officially registered Boxer of 1895 actually looked different from the modern-day Boxer. Early Boxers were stockier in build and longer in body. Within 20 years, though, the outline of the modern Boxer began to emerge.

Body Type

Today's Boxer is a medium-sized dog, with males standing 23 to 25 inches (58.4 to 63.5 cm) tall and weighing 65 to 70 pounds (29.5 to 31.8 kg). Females are usually 21 to 23 inches (53.3 to 58.4 cm) tall and weigh 55 to 60 pounds (24.9 to 27.2 kg). The breed is characterized by its *brachycephalic* head, a very short, broad head with an undershot bite. (Like the Bulldog, the Boxer's undershot bite allowed the dog to breathe through his nose while

The Expert Knows

Pioneers in the Boxer Breed

It is generally believed that the modern Boxer in America owes his existence to Frau Friederun Stockmann of Germany. Frau Stockmann and her husband, Philip, established their von Dom Kennel in the early 1900s, breeding some of the finest Boxers ever seen. Philip Stockmann and several Boxers served on the front lines during World War I, but Frau Stockmann kept the kennel going, sometimes bicycling ten miles to get food for their dogs. Of the four German foundation sires considered the cornerstones of the American Boxer, three are von Dom dogs.

holding onto his prey or opponent.) Brachycephalic dogs have a harder time regulating body temperature and are susceptible to hypothermia and heatstroke. The Boxer's short muzzle also lends itself to snoring, as any Boxer owner can attest!

Coloration

Boxers are always one of two colors: *fawn or brindle.* Fawn colors range in shades from pale tan to deep deer red, with the deeper shades more desirable. Brindle refers to a fawn background overlaid with varying black stripes. Abundant black striping that obscures

Why I Adore My Boxer

8

the fawn background gives the impression of a *reverse brindle.*

Random white markings known as *flash* cause a Boxer to be described as *flashy fawn* or *flashy brindle.* An all-white Boxer is really a fawn or brindle with very extensive white markings covering most of or the entire coat. These dogs are called *ultra-flashy,* meaning they have little or no color pigmentation. A gene responsible for extreme white spotting determines the amount of flash. *Flashy fawns* or *flashy brindles* have one copy of this gene, while *ultra-flashy* Boxers have two. A gene for deafness can also be present in white Boxers, which is why breeders will not breed them. In fact, the AKC used to prohibit white Boxers from being sold, bred, or placed as a pet. Breeders with white pups either kept them all or had them euthanized. Thankfully, this rule was repealed in the late 1990s, although breeders placing white Boxers as pets will stipulate that they be neutered. The number of websites dedicated to white Boxers proves their success as family dogs.

Temperament and Behavioral Traits

As every Boxer fancier knows, this is one of the most good-natured breeds around. Not only do they have a great love of people, but they also get along well with other pets. In addition, Boxers are extremely intelligent, trainable dogs who have a great desire to please.

At the same time, as exceptional as the Boxer is, his high intelligence and energy levels present a challenge to owners. First-time Boxer owners may be in for a few surprises, not all pleasant. The Boxer's affectionate nature may be more demanding than bargained for. His resourcefulness can get him into mischief. His athleticism may require more activity from his family members than they are able or willing to provide. Fortunately, these issues are generally avoided by prospective owners' thorough research into the breed and its characteristics.

Love of People

The Boxer's loyalty and love for his family make him a natural watchdog. Furious barking when someone approaches the door alerts the family and gives strangers pause, as well as paws. However, intruders don't need to know that Boxers are typically not human-aggressive. Should a burglar enter the house, he is more likely to be tackled, pinned, and licked into submission by the family Boxer. When a friendly visitor is invited into the home, the Boxer's barking reverts to furious tail wagging and the curling of his body into a horseshoe shape while he turns in a circle, the Boxer

FAMILY-FRIENDLY TIP

Boxers and Children

Perhaps one of the breeds best suited to children, the Boxer adores playing with kids and considers himself one of them. He senses that small children need gentler play, is stoic about the inevitable tail and ear pulls from toddlers, and is forgiving if a child accidentally falls on him. It's important, though, to teach children the following common-sense rules:

- Don't pet a sleeping dog. Wake him first by saying his name.
- Respect his crate. This is his special place and not a plaything.
- Don't pester an eating dog or try to take a bone away from him.
- Be kind and gentle to him; a dog has feelings.

hallmark of happy anticipation.

Boxers love being with their family and want to be included in all activities. This strong, exuberant dog enjoys nothing more than active play with the older children in the family. They seem to know, somehow, which family members are able to play with enthusiasm equal to their own and which should be approached gently. Even so, his very size and strength can overpower a small child. Many a toddler has been toppled by the Boxer's enthusiastic kisses. Youngsters should be supervised until they can hold their own with the dog—which won't take very long!

The even-tempered Boxer manages to keep his cool even if mistreated. National Boxer Rescue estimates that less than 1 percent of the more than 1,000 Boxers rescued were euthanized due to poor temperaments toward humans. Considering that these dogs were rescued from dire situations of abuse and/or neglect, it is surprising that the number isn't higher. This small percentage is a testament to the breed's sweet disposition. Not surprisingly, Boxers raised with loving care have an even smaller percentage of poor temperament.

Sociability With Other Pets

A home shared with one or more other pets can be a perfect outlet for the Boxer's high energy level, especially if the other pet is just as active. Two Boxers can romp together for hours, long after they have worn you out. And a canine companion for your Boxer reduces the chances of his becoming bored and mischievous.

If you decide to add another Boxer—or any other dog—to your

Boxers are social animals who love being with their human family.

family, it is a good idea to try for the opposite sex. Some Boxers tend to be dog-aggressive, and there is less likely to be a dominance issue with a female-male pairing. That's not to say that two males, (particularly if they're neutered) or two females can't live in harmony with each other. However, if any animosity toward the other dog develops, regardless of gender, the Boxer is capable of holding a lifelong grudge that necessitates permanent separation. A determined owner will usually make the effort required to separate them within the same household, but in extreme cases where there is a threat of serious injury to each other, a new home for one of them may be the only solution.

If you are bringing a Boxer puppy home to pets of other species—cats, birds, rabbits—chances are that he will learn to respect them and live happily together. Cats with intact claws have little trouble putting even an adult Boxer in his place when necessary. Smaller pets, like hamsters, gerbils, and mice, should be introduced to a puppy with supervision. The dog's instincts may tell him that the guinea pig in your hand is prey or a new toy, rather than a fellow family pet.

Intelligence

The Boxer's intelligence makes him a very trainable dog who thoroughly enjoys any opportunity to be with his owner. His desire to please is evident in

Famous Boxer Owners

- Shirley Temple
- Humphrey Bogart and Lauren Bacall
- Nat King Cole
- Joe DiMaggio
- Sylvester Stallone
- Ice-T
- Jodie Foster
- Pablo Picasso
- David Niven
- Steffi Graf
- Dian Fossey
- Emily Bronte
- Charlton Heston
- Janet Jackson

how quickly he learns, and his versatility and athletic prowess make him an ideal candidate for a variety of dog sports. His compliant nature is a good foundation for advanced competition requiring strict obedience, like agility and Schutzhund, a rigorous trial of tracking, obedience, and protection.

Trainability

Boxers aren't large dogs, but they are powerful and often don't know their own strength. An adolescent Boxer can

SENIOR DOG TIP

The "Silver" Boxer

A sad fact about dog ownership is that they aren't with us very long. An average Boxer lives about 9 to 13 years, and he is considered a senior at age 7. Often called "silver Boxers" because of the gray hair that turns their face and coat silvery, aging Boxers may tire more quickly and sleep a little more.

To care for your aging Boxer, keep an eye on his teeth and gums, and let his stamina level be your guide to exercise. A healthy lifestyle of wholesome food, moderate exercise, and lots of love will increase his chances of a long and happy life with you.

knock a visitor off balance in his excitement to greet him, or pull on the leash so hard that his walk turns into your jog. Obedience training should begin as soon as your vet gives the green light for a puppy class, usually after your dog has received all of his shots. This "kindergarten" socializes the puppy and teaches him the basics he will need in order to further his schooling. Puppy classes also teach the Boxer how to interact acceptably with other dogs and people.

Physical Activity

To a Boxer, any time is playtime. He doesn't just want to hang out; he wants to play with you. Boxers won't always settle for a lackadaisical toss of the ball, either—they want you to chase them for the ball. A bored Boxer will either pester you by whining and clinging or else find his own source of entertainment, perhaps chewing on something he shouldn't. An adequately exercised Boxer enjoys a morning romp, a midday walk, and some evening play. If you don't have a fenced yard for him to play in, you must take him on some vigorous walks or light runs.

Need for Companionship

All dogs are social animals, and Boxers are especially so. They adore their humans and do not want to be apart from them for very long. When dealing with your absence, your Boxer may come up with ways to amuse himself that you don't find amusing, such as digging up the flower beds or chewing on that new chair leg.

Boxers are also talented escape artists and may try to get out of the yard to rejoin the family. For this reason, backyard fencing should be at least 6 feet (1.8 m) high and reinforced below ground to prevent him from

Boxers are active dogs who enjoy a great deal of physical activity.

copiously when excited or tantalized by something particularly yummy. Then there's the flatulence—Boxers seem bent on sharing their personal perfume. They won't care that your new boss is over for dinner or that you've just finished teaching your child that passing gas in public is a no-no. Most Boxer owners are able to accept these habits, and they learn to just go with the flow.

Boxers also harbor a stubborn streak a mile wide that first appears in these dogs when they are mature. If you aren't committed to working through it, you could end up with a dog who tends to dominate his owner. This doesn't mean that he'll become aggressive toward you, but he will know that he has the upper hand. Most instances of a Boxer causing household upheaval can be resolved with patience, creativity, and a willingness to adapt your lifestyle to accommodate the Boxer's needs.

To a Boxer, the glass is always half full, a good philosophy for us to follow. There's a popular joke that asks, "How many Boxers does it take to screw in a lightbulb?" The answer is, "Who cares? I can still play with my squeaky toy in the dark."

With an attitude like that, who can help but smile?

digging his way out. If you have considered an electronic containment system, keep in mind that they do not keep other animals or people from entering your yard. If your Boxer is sufficiently motivated to escape, he'll brave the slight electric shock he receives when breaching the confinement area.

Unpleasant Traits

The Boxer does have a few socially unappealing habits. Those pendulous upper lips make him somewhat of a messy eater and drinker. He can drool

Chapter 2

The Stuff of
Everyday
Life

Just as new parents stock up on baby essentials, so should you prepare when bringing home a new Boxer. Necessities like nutritious puppy food, safe and age-appropriate dog toys, and a comfortable crate should be ready and waiting for the newest family member. You should also puppy proof the home environment, removing anything that poses a safety hazard. Your commitment to keeping your Boxer happy and healthy takes effort, but your reward will be a long life together.

A little advance planning can ease your dog's transition into the family. Let's discuss a few essentials you will need to purchase before you welcome your new Boxer home.

Crate

Dogs are den animals who feel secure in a protected or sheltered area. An appropriately sized crate provides this safe haven for your Boxer and is an important housetraining tool.

A proper-size crate should be big enough for the dog to sit, stand, and turn around comfortably yet small enough so that he can't soil it without compromising his sleeping area. This means that you will have to upgrade the crate size a couple of times during your Boxer's growth. Another option is to buy a crate large enough for an adult Boxer and partition off half of it. (The average adult Boxer is comfortable in a crate approximately 24 inches [61.0 cm] wide, 36 inches [91.4 cm] long, and 28 inches [71.1 cm] high.) Relocate the partition as

he grows. The crate will remain your adult Boxer's own special nook, a place where he can retreat from the commotion of the household but still stay with his "pack."

Exercise Pen

An exercise pen is a crating alternative that confines the dog but offers more

An exercise pen is a crating alternative that confines a dog but offers more freedom.

freedom. Boxer owners unable to fence in the yard for their dog(s) often compromise by erecting an exercise pen within the yard. The dimensions can vary, but the pen should be large enough to allow roaming room.

Indoors, exercise pens are really puppy playpens. Breeders use them to confine litters to a safe, warm area when the pups' mother is not around. A pen also gives your puppy a little freedom but keeps him safe while you are on the phone or cooking dinner. As mentioned in Chapter 1, Boxers are accomplished escape artists, so don't be lulled into a false sense of security. After a period of time, unsupervised penned puppies are going to take on the challenge of busting out of the joint, risking their safety and your home's order. Keep your dog in a pen only when you are at home and can get to him readily.

Baby Gates

Like the pen, a baby gate affords your dog some freedom but prevents him from wandering into uncharted territory. A baby gate is also assembly-free and inexpensive. Gated-off stairways prevent falls, and gated rooms confine your dog to a specific area.

Gates are not infallible, though. The fearless Boxer puppy who figures out that it makes a great climbing wall can get his head caught in the nylon latticework or tumble off the top.

FAMILY-FRIENDLY TIP

Children as Caregivers

It is important to teach your children that your Boxer is part of the family and deserving of the same respect, love, and care as any family member. Teaching them about the responsibility that comes with dog ownership is valuable, but young children may not have the maturity to handle that much responsibility. You wouldn't leave an infant with a ten-year-old babysitter, nor should you leave a puppy with a ten-year-old child in charge. Appropriate behavior and responsibility should be taught to children with the guidance of a competent adult.

Stick to crating when you are away from the home.

Dog Bed

Your Boxer loves to relax in his crate near the family, but what if the family is gathered elsewhere in the house? Several inexpensive dog beds mean that he can always be comfortably near. Whichever style you choose, make sure the filling is well contained within the bed. If your impish Boxer chews through the fabric, you don't want

Doggy Day Care

Dogs are social animals who shouldn't be left alone for long periods of time. Aside from social interaction, your Boxer will need to be fed, watered, allowed to eliminate, and exercised while the family is at school and work. What are your options?

- *Doggy day care programs:* They will "interview" your Boxer for suitability and provide first-rate care while he enjoys the companionship of other dogs. Only well-trained and socialized Boxers need apply.
- *Professional (bonded and insured) dog walkers or pet sitters:* They allow your Boxer to remain in the comfort of his own home.
- *Responsible neighbors:* This means an adult to whom you can entrust the well-being of your Boxer, not a child looking to make enough cash for the latest video game.
- *Relatives or friends willing to help out:* If they have the experience and the desire, lucky you!

feathers, cedar chips, or beans spilled out everywhere, much less ingested by your dog.

Food and Water Bowls

Food and water bowls commonly come in plastic, stainless steel, and ceramic. If you purchase special bowls made of any exotic material, ask the vet about possible adverse interactions with ingredients in your dog's food that can make him sick. Plastic dog dishes can cause an allergic skin reaction, and ceramics break easily, so stainless steel is your best bet.

Collar

For everyday use, an adjustable, flat nylon buckle collar is best. It should fit comfortably

Food and water bowls made of stainless steel are a sturdy, hygienic choice for your Boxer.

around the Boxer's neck, not so loose that he can wriggle out of it and not so tight that it constricts his throat. The nylon show collar should be used for training sessions only, as it has no spot for identification. Chain collars are not advisable, as they can easily catch on something and cause injury or even strangle the dog. Prong and pinch collars are not recommended and in some areas are not allowed. Be sure your contact information is stitched or permanently written into the collar or on attached identification tags.

Leash

Leashes (or *leads*) come in a wide variety of lengths, materials, and purposes. Puppies will naturally follow you off lead, but they need leashes for basic training. Purchase one that is about 5 (1.5 m) or 6 feet (1.8 m) long and made of a strong, flexible fabric like nylon, cotton webbing, or leather. Once your dog is comfortable with controlled leash walks, you can switch to a different type or length and use the long one just for training. Retractable leashes are popular, but be sure you get the right size for the strong Boxer.

Grooming Supplies

The Boxer's short, sleek coat requires minimal care to keep it looking gorgeous. A few

The Expert Knows

Setting Up a Schedule

Dogs thrive on routine, so you will want to establish one for your Boxer as soon as possible. The sooner he knows what to expect and when, the easier he will settle into your household. Feedings, eliminations, playtime, and bedtime should all be done as regularly as possible to facilitate housetraining and to give your dog a sense of security.

19

purchased supplies combined with others you already have at home, and you're good to go.

Brushing

For grooming to become a treat for your Boxer, introduce it to him early. Daily sessions with a soft brush will teach your puppy that grooming is relaxing for him and good bonding time for both of you. Short hair notwithstanding, Boxers do shed, and old hair needs to be removed. Brushing also stimulates circulation and sloughs off dead skin cells. Regular brushing distributes natural skin oils throughout the coat, keeping it shiny.

Boxers "blow their coat" twice yearly: in spring, to get rid of dead hair

The Stuff of Everyday Life

and make room for new growth, and in fall, when their winter coat thickens up and loosens older, dead hair. A fine-tooth shedding comb catches the molting undercoat in its fine teeth along the entire edge. Shedding combs have larger teeth on one edge, but the fine-tooth edge is all that your Boxer's coat needs.

Bathing

Boxers are naturally clean dogs who groom themselves like cats. Regular brushing also keeps them clean, so Boxers don't need regular baths. Excessive bathing strips natural skin oils and promotes itchy, dry skin. Unless your Boxer rolls around in something nasty or goes out for mud wrestling, he won't need regular baths. If you feel strongly about it, try not to bathe your Boxer more frequently than once a month in summer and once every two months in

The Boxer's short, sleek coat requires minimal care to keep it looking shiny and healthy.

winter. Use only a mild dog shampoo, because human shampoos have too much detergent that can irritate his skin and eyes. Finally, keep in mind that the bathing area you select should be warm.

Dental Care

Dogs in the wild keep their teeth and gums clean naturally, but Boxers need a

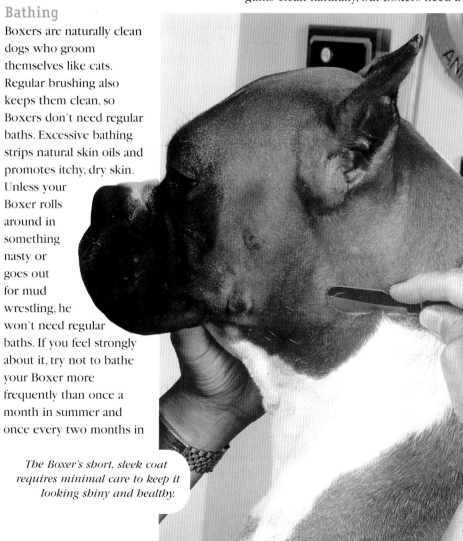

Licensing in Your State or Municipality

One of the most important steps you can take toward responsible Boxer ownership is to research any local legislation that will affect you. Find out if pet dogs must be registered with the county or city. More important, find out if there is any breed-specific legislation. Many communities have laws against owning certain breeds deemed "vicious." This usually calls to mind the "pit bull," the catchall moniker used to refer to any dog breeds or mixes descended from ancient fighting dogs. This may include American Pit Bull Terriers, American Staffordshire Terriers, Staffordshire Bull Terriers, Bull Terriers, and yes, Boxers. Mere physical resemblance to a "pit bull" is sometimes all it takes for a dog to be banned. If you live in such an area and think you can elude the law, you run the risk of having your Boxer confiscated and/or killed. Investigate the law *before* bringing your Boxer home.

little human help to keep their mouths healthy. Crunchy dog food and chew toys clean teeth and gums somewhat, but they won't prevent tartar buildup that could lead to periodontal disease. Left untreated, infections in the mouth can travel through the bloodstream and attack vital organs. This is why it is worth the effort to brush your Boxer's teeth with a soft toothbrush or a finger sheath. Use only dog toothpaste, as human toothpaste isn't intended for consumption, and dogs don't know how to spit it out.

Identification

Sometimes the unthinkable happens. Your dog runs off, gets lost, or is even abducted. (Stolen dogs are often sold for fighting or as lab test subjects.) Your Boxer is too precious to lose, so make sure he is always identifiable.

Tags

ID tags are the easiest way to identify dogs. In addition to the legally required rabies vaccination tag, your Boxer should have a tag bearing his name, your name and address, and your

Your Boxer's collar should fit comfortably around his neck.

A Sound Mind in a Sound Body

As with people, regular frequent exercise is important to your dog's physical and emotional well-being. The athletic Boxer needs to *run,* not stroll, and play hard to keep his beautiful physique and mental acuity. Take him for a brisk walk or a jog, play fetch in an enclosed tennis court, or just play tag. The exercise will do you good, too!

telephone number. If you live where dog registration is required by law, he'll be issued a tag with his registration number. Never let him outdoors unless he's wearing his collar and tags. They may save his life.

Microchipping

A tiny capsule about the size of a long grain of rice, the microchip is injected under a skin flap on the back of a dog's neck. The capsule contains a numbered chip that the dog owner lists with an international dog registry. When a lost dog is turned in to a shelter or veterinarian, he is scanned for this microchip, the number is read, and it is called in to the registry for contact information.

Microchipping is painless and permanent and can never be altered, making it an extremely reliable means of identification. Abducted or stray dogs who end up in experimental laboratories are scanned for microchips and returned to their owners unharmed.

Toys

Part of the fun that you will have as a new Boxer owner will be selecting some toys. The key is to choose toys that are age appropriate and safe. Rubbery squeaky toys are favorites of Boxers, who are known to vocalize with them. But monitor the dog's play with them, as the rubber or plastic is easily torn, and an unsupervised puppy could swallow pieces or choke on the squeaker. The same goes for stuffed toys. Shredding a stuffed toy

Provide safe, age-appropriate toys for your Boxer.

can entertain a Boxer for hours, but he doesn't need this kind of fiber in his diet. Avoid stuffed toys with buttons or other small appliquéd decorations that present choking hazards.

Puppies especially, of course, but Boxers in general have a lifelong need to chew. The ideal chew toy is one that can stand up to rigorous use but is not so hard or brittle that it can injure the dog.

Hard nylon "bones" with flavor coating or teeth-cleaning texture are made to withstand chewing without splintering. Splintered pieces of real animal bone or flimsy artificial material can cause serious internal injury if swallowed. Replace chew toys that are roughened or shredded, and avoid chew treats like rawhide and pigs' ears. Dogs love them, but their indigestibility can cause injury or intestinal blockage. The same is true of cow hooves, another favorite. The brittle hooves splinter easily, and the sharp pieces can puncture internal organs and tissue.

Bringing a Boxer home means that your life will never be the same. Your

SENIOR DOG TIP

Adopting the Older Boxer

With so many dogs rescued each year from abusive or neglectful homes, you may want to consider adopting an adult or senior Boxer. True, you will miss the adorable, cuddly puppy stage, but you will also miss chewing, housetraining, crate training, and teething. Giving a loving home to an adult Boxer can be a fulfilling, albeit challenging, experience that may include problem behaviors, fear, depression, and health issues. Older dogs should be adopted only if owners have the patience, love, and financial means to properly care for them. Support provided by rescue programs, behavioral specialists, and other Boxer owners can help you move past any rough spots.

household routine will be disrupted, your home a little dirtier, your expenses a little higher. However, you will also receive unconditional love, endless entertainment, and a guardian for life. What more could you ask for?

Chapter 3

Good
Eating

Long ago, humankind made a commitment to
provide for dogs what dogs once got for
themselves—nourishing food. Unless there's some
wild boar roaming in the nearby woods, it's up to
the Boxer owner to make sure that he has a
balanced diet of good-quality food.

Food Basics

Dogs in the wild are omnivores, meaning they meet nutritional needs by eating both plant and animal matter.

This may be surprising, as dogs are usually considered carnivores, or meat-eaters only. When a wild dog kills a prey animal, he consumes every part of that animal, including the stomach and its contents. The meat provides protein, the bones provide essential minerals, and the digestive tract of herbivorous prey provides the small amount of vegetable matter he needs to round out his diet.

Wholesome dog food containing the right amounts of proteins, carbohydrates, fats, vitamins, and minerals will help keep your Boxer looking and feeling his best, as will the right amount of water.

Proteins

Protein is important for bone growth, tissue healing, and the daily replacement of spent body tissues. All animal tissue has a high protein level, but

Wholesome dog food will keep your dog looking and feeling his best.

because protein isn't stored in the body, a dog must get it from food every day of his life.

Fats

Fat is used as an energy source and keeps your Boxer's skin and coat healthy and shiny. Eating the right balance of fats is important. Too much fat results in obesity and can lead to other health problems. Insufficient fat can cause itchy skin, a dull coat, dandruff, and even ear infections. Dietary fats help protect the short-coated Boxer from extreme cold and also make his food tasty.

Carbohydrates

Carbohydrates aid digestion and elimination and are comprised of sugars, starch, and cellulose. About five percent of a Boxer's complete diet should be fiber from carbohydrates, necessitating some plant consumption. Good sources include boiled potatoes, carrots, rice, and whole grains. Excess carbohydrates are stored in the body for later use, but it is hard to imagine an active Boxer with many carbohydrates to spare.

Vitamins

Vitamins are organic compounds that function as metabolic regulators in the body. A balanced diet should provide all the vitamins your Boxer needs. Supplements should be given only under vet supervision, because it is easy to overdose and create health problems where there were none.

Vitamin A

Vitamin A is used for fat absorption and promotes good eyesight, normal growth rate, and healthy reproduction.

B Vitamins

B vitamins are important for coat, skin, appetite, growth, and eyes. They also protect the nervous system and aid metabolism.

Vitamin C

Vitamin C is synthesized in a dog's liver, so it is not usually added to a dog's diet.

Vitamin D

Vitamin D is essential for healthy bones, teeth, and muscle tone, but it must be taken with the proper ratio of calcium and phosphorus.

Vitamin E

Vitamin E promotes proper muscle function, internal and reproductive organ function, and all cell membrane function.

SENIOR DOG TIP

Feeding the Older Boxer

A dog's metabolism slows with age, and the aging rate can vary from dog to dog. By the time a Boxer is seven, he is considered a senior citizen. His interest in food may wane for a variety of reasons. Dental problems can make mealtime a painful experience, and your vet should be consulted. If your Boxer's senses have dulled, he may become a picky eater. You can try warming his food to make it smell more appetizing or dividing it up into smaller amounts to offer throughout the day. Just the change alone may entice a fussy eater.

Geriatric Boxers need food with a lower percentage of protein than they did in their prime. On average, senior Boxers should eat 20 percent fewer calories. Senior-formula dog foods are manufactured with this in mind. They also have less fat and added nutrients for age-related health problems like arthritis. Check labels to compare ingredients.

Good Eating

The Expert Knows

Table Manners

Nobody likes sitting down to dinner with a whining dog or having one's cookies stolen. This is why teaching your Boxer good manners around food is important for his health and social acceptability.

Vitamin K

Vitamin K is synthesized in the digestive tract, so like vitamin C, it is not usually added to a dog's diet.

Minerals

Minerals are nutritional elements obtained from food. The following are some of the most common minerals:

- **Calcium and phosphorus**: In the correct ratio, calcium and phosphorus work together to prevent rickets and other bone deformities. They also aid in tooth formation, muscle development, and lactation in nursing bitches.
- **Potassium**: Contributes to normal growth and healthy nerves and muscles.

- **Sodium** and **chlorine**: Help maintain appetite and normal activity level.
- **Magnesium**: Helps synthesize proteins, as well as prevent convulsions and nervous system problems.
- **Iron**: Needed for healthy blood, aided by **copper**.
- **Iodine**: Prevents goiter (enlarged thyroid).
- **Zinc**: Promotes healthy skin.
- **Cobalt**: Aids normal growth and keeps the reproductive tract sound, aided by **manganese**.

As with vitamins, supplement minerals only under your veterinarian's advice.

Water

Proper hydration is the trend these days; everyone you see carries a bottle of spring water. Your Boxer doesn't need a popular brand of purchased water, but he does need

Your Boxer should receive plenty of cool, fresh water to drink throughout the day.

Reading and Understanding Food Labels

How can you be sure you're selecting the right food for your Boxer? It's all there on the label, once you know what to look for. A label that says "100% nutritionally complete" means that the food is appropriate for dogs in any life stage. References like "puppy" or "senior" mean that the food is designed especially for the nutritional needs of that phase. For example, senior-formula dog foods may be lower in calories and have added mineral supplements. Puppy kibble may be smaller and finer in texture, which is easier on a puppy's immature digestive system.

Labels often have a *guaranteed analysis* chart that breaks down levels of protein, fat, fiber, and moisture in the food. This is nice-to-know information, but it doesn't say much about the quality of the food. The nutritional value of the ingredients is what really matters.

lots of cool, fresh water to drink throughout the day, every day. A healthy dog should consume (from food and drink) ½ (14.8 ml) to ¾ fluid ounce (22.2 ml) per pound (0.45 kg) of body weight per day. In hot weather and after exercise, he will need more. Excessive thirst can be a symptom of illness, so check with the vet if you notice that your dog is drinking more than usual.

Types of Dog Food

More so than in decades past, we are aware of our dogs' dietary needs and the best ways to meet them. Quality, cost, and convenience should be considered in planning your Boxer's diet. Understanding the nutritional breakdown listed on dog food labels is also important for making good food choices for the Boxer in your life.

Commercial Foods

Commercial dog food reigns as the most popular way to feed the family dog, and there are dozens of available products to prove it. Happily, dog food companies have made great strides in improving product quality. They also recognize the different nutritional needs at different life stages with foods formulated specifically for puppies, healthy adult dogs, overweight dogs, and senior citizens. Beware of foods listing "animal by-products" as their primary ingredient, which are animal parts with little or no nutritional value, like ground-up hooves and beaks.

Keep in mind that the healthiest dog foods are not always conveniently sold at supermarkets. You may have to make a trip to a specialty store, but isn't your Boxer worth it?

Dry food, or kibble, helps reduce tartar buildup on a dog's teeth.

Canned Food (Wet)

Canned dog food smells and tastes great to Boxers. It has a long shelf life and is widely available at supermarkets and convenience stores. However, it can be the most expensive food option, and it does little for a Boxer's oral hygiene. The soft consistency of the food doesn't provide the teeth-cleaning action of dry food and can contribute to bad breath. Be discriminating. Select a canned food that is high in protein and low in filler (processed grains), water, and fat.

Semi-Moist Food

Semi-moist foods come in meaty-looking shapes, but they are usually the least healthy of all commercial types, filled with artificial color, flavor, and aroma. While it doesn't cut it as an exclusive diet, this type of food makes tasty occasional treats.

Noncommercial Foods

With proper research and preparation, a fresh diet is an excellent way to make sure your Boxer is eating right. It will have few, if any, chemicals or preservatives, and plenty of good-quality ingredients tailored to your Boxer's needs. But providing your Boxer with a noncommercial diet is a commitment that takes time, education, and

Dry Food (Kibble)

A popular, economical choice, dry dog food keeps well without refrigeration and can be bought in bulk quantities. It also helps reduce tartar buildup on your dog's teeth. On the down side, dry foods usually have more preservatives than other types. Ingested kibble expands in the stomach, which might be a problem for breeds predisposed to gastric torsion.

Ingredients are listed on the package in order of predominance, from greatest to least. A wholesome source of digestible protein (lamb, chicken, beef, or fish) should be one of the first four. Healthy secondary ingredients include rice, whole grains, cottage cheese, fruits, and/or vegetables.

dedication, lest you shortchange your Boxer's nutrition. If you are willing to put forth the time and effort, your dog's glowing good health will be your reward.

The Home-Cooked Diet

The numbers of dog owners who feed only home-cooked food have actually dwindled in the last 20 years due to the improvement in commercial food quality, but those loyal to home preparation swear by it. It can be labor intensive, but after a while, you'll have the process down to a science and prep time to a minimum.

A home-cooked diet usually consists of cooked chicken or meat with some cooked whole-grain oatmeal or cottage cheese. Vegetables can be added according to your Boxer's preferences. Some common human foods, like chocolate, onions, and macadamia nuts, to name a few, are toxic to dogs, so ask your vet for guidance. Do your research so that you become an expert in canine nutrition.

The Raw Diet

A contemporary dog's digestive system is pretty much the same as it was thousands of years ago, consisting of a short intestinal tract and strong stomach acids for consuming and digesting raw food. Many people believe that dogs should eat the way nature intended, and so they opt for a BARF (**b**iologically **a**ppropriate **r**aw **f**ood) diet. BARF diets have long been common practice in Europe, especially in Germany. A once-skeptical United States seems to have put into perspective its fear of bacteria and parasite infection, making a full-fledged BARF movement out of an underground fad.

Common-sense precautions, like thawing frozen meat in the refrigerator instead of at room temperature, lessen the risk of bacteria. In addition, there is a greater chance of contracting parasites from wild prey than from properly handled, human-grade

If you are willing to put forth the time and effort to provide your dog with a noncommercial diet, your dog's glowing good health will be your reward.

FAMILY-FRIENDLY TIP

Children and Dog Feeding

Teaching children compassion and responsibility for animals can never start too early, and your Boxer can be a great teacher's aide. Children who are five years of age and older are able and usually eager to take part in activities surrounding the family dog. Let your child portion out the kibble into the dog's bowl or blend together a wet and dry mixture. It can fall to older children to make sure that your Boxer always has clean, cool drinking water, or to give an after-dinner treat.

Try to find tasks that are age appropriate for both child and dog. An eager-to-eat adolescent Boxer could topple over a four-year-old carrying a food dish, or at the very least, spill it. A youngster should offer a treat from the palm of her hand so that little fingers aren't accidentally nipped.

Be vigilant in supervising dogs and kids, especially at mealtime. Very young children may be tempted to taste Rover's dinner, which can result in stomach upset and/or a nipped hand. Instruct children never to bother a dog who is eating.

meat. (An exception is pork, which can transmit the *Trichinella* parasite.)

Raw food should be left raw. Microwaving even as briefly as 30 seconds damages live enzymes and hardens the bones. And speaking of bones, remember the commandment *Thou shalt not give thy dog chicken bones?* More specifically, *cooked* poultry bones are dangerous. *Raw* bones don't splinter; they crunch into small pieces that help clean the teeth. They are also a good source of calcium and phosphorus.

There are no magic cures for physical ailments, but many BARFers think a raw diet is the next best thing. Allergies and other skin conditions, chronic ear and gastrointestinal conditions, and bad breath often disappear after transitioning to a raw diet. If you want your Boxer to go raw, consult your veterinarian.

Types of Feeding Schedules

Just like human babies, puppies eat frequent small meals. In between naps and playtime, they will consume about four meals a day. The amount varies with each dog, but Boxer puppies should have about ¼ cup (59.1 ml) of food at each meal. As puppies grow, meals will become less frequent and proportionately bigger. Your vet or breeder can offer guidance on meal portions and frequency.

There are basically two ways to nourish your Boxer: free feeding and scheduled feeding. As the name implies, free feeding means unlimited food available all the time. Scheduled feeding is done at one or more predetermined regular times during the day. Common sense says that an appropriate amount of food at specific intervals is the healthy way to feed your Boxer. To decide for yourself, take a look at both ways.

Scheduled Feeding

If your lifestyle takes you away from home during the day while your Boxer is still a puppy, someone must come over a few times a day to feed him and take him outside. This multi-meal schedule will continue for several months, and you will need to accommodate it.

To keep the "scheduled" in scheduled feeding, limit the length of mealtime. No picky eating allowed! If your dog doesn't eat all of his food immediately, take it away after 10 or 15 minutes. He will quickly

With scheduled feeding, your dog must eat all of his food immediately or wait until his next scheduled meal.

figure out that he must take advantage of this window of opportunity to eat, or wait until the next scheduled meal.

Scheduled feeding helps regulate elimination, which makes housetraining easier. If your Boxer is taken outside to eliminate after every meal, the housetraining message will be reinforced. Scheduled meals also mean less chance of digestive upsets. Your Boxer is less likely to gulp his food, a bad habit that can lead to gastric torsion, a dangerous and often fatal condition.

Free Feeding

You've heard of those elaborate midnight buffets on cruise ships. Imagine having one at home, around the clock, every day of the week. That's what free feeding amounts to. Most dogs won't stop eating when they feel full, so a free-feeding Boxer is likely to become overweight, lethargic, and unenthusiastic about his food, an impediment to obedience training. What Boxer would be tempted by a treat when life is one endless midnight buffet?

A dog's digestive system is not designed for continuous, unlimited eating. Dogs in the wild have long interludes between meals, which give their bodies a chance to rest after digestion and prepare for the next meal. Free feeding can also lead to begging, a trick your Boxer doesn't need in his repertoire. If his food is available all the time, he's going to get bored with it. The burgers on the grill will tantalize him much more than the same old stuff in his dish. He may ignore his food completely and wait at the dinner table for handouts. Not only is this a bad habit, but it may not provide him with sufficient nutrition. The only thing he should have available at all times is fresh, cool water.

In short, the only advantage to free feeding is that it sets *you* free from making a trip home to feed the dog. It doesn't do your Boxer any good. Even if he doesn't gobble his food down all at once, it will sit out for a long period of time, becoming unappetizing and possibly spoiled. Is your personal freedom worth compromising your Boxer's health?

Obesity

A healthy adult male Boxer weighs between 65 (29.5 kg) and 80 pounds (36.3 kg), and females are about 15 pounds (6.8 kg) lighter. The actual number is less important than the ratio

Feeding Chart

Feeding charts are handy for figuring out the right amount of food for your Boxer. Many dog food companies print them on their packaging for easy reference. The parameters in this sample chart are based on an average Boxer's weight. Total caloric intake should come from quality food that meets the dog's complete nutritional needs.

Sample Feeding Schedule for Each Phase of Your Boxer's Life

	Puppies: weaning to 3 months	Adolescents: 4 to 12 months	Active Adults: 1 to 7 years	Sedentary Adults: more than 2 years	Senior Citizens: 8 years and older
Times per Day	four	three	one or two	two	one or two
Amount per Meal	1/4 cup (59.1 ml)	1/3 cup (78.9 ml)	1 cup (236.6 ml)	3/4 (177.4 ml) to 1 cup (236.6 ml)	3/4 (177.4 ml) to 1 cup (236.6 ml)
Best Food	puppy formula	puppy formula	adult maintenance formula	overweight adult or senior formula	senior formula

of weight to size. But the Boxer's some-what stocky physique can mask a few extra pounds (kg), so how do you know if yours is at an appropriate weight?

Every veterinary visit, regardless of the reason, will chart your Boxer's current weight, so you should already have an idea of his poundage. In between visits, you can eyeball his weight by running your hands lightly along his sides. If you can feel his ribs without exerting pressure, his weight is probably fine. If they are hidden underneath excess fat and you have to press down to feel them, he is probably overweight. Also, observe his energy level. A fit Boxer prances around, always ready to play. A couch potato moves sluggishly and tires quickly.

At some point during the aging process, your Boxer's metabolism will slow down. If you don't reduce his food intake accordingly, he'll gain weight. An overweight Boxer is an unhealthy dog. Obesity stresses joints and forces internal organs to work harder. The "food is love" motto makes no more sense for your Boxer than it does for your human family members. Saying no to junk food and too many treats is a better way to show your love. Make sure that he gets plenty of exercise to keep his beautiful body in shape.

Proper nutrition is crucial to a dog's well-being. It keeps him feeling and looking good and helps prevent disease by keeping his immune system working at full throttle. The more you know about canine nutrition, the easier it will be to feed your Boxer what he needs and enjoys. "Bone" appétit!

Chapter 4

Looking Good

No one can argue that the Boxer is one of the handsomest dog breeds around. The sleek coat, chiseled physique, and lively, intelligent eyes all add up to a dog who turns heads. And it doesn't take a lot of time and money to keep him that way. Regular grooming does more than beautify your Boxer. It's the perfect opportunity for you to spend quality time together. Gentle brushing or combing is really just petting with a purpose.

As far as your Boxer is concerned, it doesn't matter if you're grooming or not. All he knows is that you're lavishing attention on him, and it feels great. With a minimum of regular care, you can bond with your Boxer and keep him looking gorgeous.

Coat and Skin Care

Your Boxer's coat does more than just give your vacuum cleaner a job. It protects his skin from the elements and helps keep him warm in cold temperatures. It's also a barometer of his general health. A Boxer in good health has a glossy, clean-smelling coat.

A dull, lackluster coat, with or without dandruff, may indicate a dietary deficiency or some other medical problem. Bald patches are a sure sign of trouble, usually mange or another skin ailment.

Checking the Skin

Grooming provides a great opportunity to give your Boxer the once-over for ticks, fleas, or lesions. Since his hair lies close to the skin, any problems reveal themselves by disrupting the smooth surface of his coat. Short hair facilitates the detection of skin irregularities when you run your hands over his body.

A Boxer in good health has a glossy, clean-smelling coat.

You'll also want to check your Boxer's skin for "hot spots," irritated or itchy places that cause the dog to repeatedly lick, scratch, or bite at the area. Even a summer heat rash can make him uncomfortable, so don't hesitate to see the veterinarian if you notice something suspicious. In the winter, a Boxer can develop dry skin and/or dandruff that dulls his coat. Omega-3 and omega-6 fatty acids, found in canola, safflower, flax, and certain other oils, help relieve dry-skin problems and come in convenient gelcaps that you can toss in with his dinner, with your vet's approval, of course. If you don't see improvement after a month, consult with your vet.

Brushing

Even though matting and tangling aren't issues for a Boxer, brushing should be a part of his regular grooming care. It stimulates circulation and distributes the natural oils that protect him against the elements.

How to Brush Your Boxer

Brushing a Boxer is a snap. All you need is a long-handled brush with dense, soft bristles or a grooming (currying) glove. (Some professional groomers prefer brushes with natural bristles, claiming that synthetic brushes generate too much static electricity.) Start at the head and follow the direction of the fur, working back toward the tail. Apply enough pressure to stimulate the skin

Grooming Supplies

The minimalist Boxer requires only a few basics:

- soft-bristle brush
- shedding comb
- sturdy pair of toenail clippers (guillotine style for puppies, shears style for adults)
- mild dog shampoo
- cotton balls
- mineral oil
- styptic powder or cornstarch

but not so much that your dog is uncomfortable. Be extra gentle on the sensitive belly and undersides where hair is sparse or on any ticklish spots that make his skin twitch.

During molting times (usually spring and fall), a shedding comb is a handy tool to have around. A metal loop fitted into a handle, the comb has a serrated edge that catches the loose undercoat. One side has small, fine teeth and the other has larger, more widely spaced teeth. The smaller side works best on a Boxer. Considering the gobs of loose hair that cling to the comb, you may want to do this bit of grooming outside.

Looking Good

Bathing

A Boxer won't need much bathing during his lifetime. Unless he's been into something dirty or is a therapy dog (many organizations require their therapy dogs to be bathed prior to every visit), a bath won't clean anything that regular brushing doesn't remove. Too much bathing strips the skin of natural oils and can lead to itching or a rash. If you feel strongly about regular bathing, keep it down to once a month in summer and once every two months in winter. Use only a mild dog shampoo. Human shampoos contain too much detergent and are harsh on a dog's skin.

Boxers are not natural water lovers, but they will stoically endure a bath to please you. The easier you make bath time, the more cooperative your Boxer will be. Even if he enjoys the water, a bath is not the same as a dip at the old swimming hole. A little organization will make the experience a nonevent.

How to Bathe Your Boxer

For an indoor bath, choose a warm location that is free from drafts.

When the water is at a comfortably warm temperature, fill the tub with just enough to cover your dog's feet. Don't fill it all the way, as you would for your own bath; your Boxer's footing will feel more secure in just a few inches (cm) of water. Lift him into the tub by wrapping one arm around his chest and the other around the back of his legs, just below the tail. Boxers are solid dogs, so you may want to enlist someone's help if you are unable to lift your dog comfortably by yourself.

When using a brush or grooming glove, apply enough pressure to stimulate the skin but not so much that your dog is uncomfortable.

Once he's in the tub, give him a minute or two to adjust to the situation. He won't enjoy being doused before he knows what hit him. Keep a hand on him at all times to make him feel secure and prevent him from jumping out. If you have a handheld shower attachment, use a soft spray to wet his body. If not, use a plastic cup or bowl to scoop up water to wet down the coat, avoiding his head. Pour a small amount of shampoo into your hand and gently work it into his coat. Take care not to get any into his ears, eyes, nose, or mouth. Not only will the shampoo irritate those areas, but it will make an unpleasant memory that can make future baths a struggle.

After shampooing your Boxer's body, use a washcloth to gently wipe his face. Wipe the inside of his ear with a cotton ball dipped in mineral oil. Never insert anything into the inner ear that could damage delicate tissues. If soap gets into his eyes, ease the sting with a drop or two of mineral oil in the corner of each eye.

Take time to rinse him thoroughly with the spray attachment or plastic cup. Soap residue will leave your Boxer's coat dull and make his skin itch. Rinsing his underside can be a challenge without a spray attachment, but make the effort to remove all traces of shampoo. When he's ready to be lifted out of the tub, get ready for your own shower, because the first thing your Boxer will do is share his personal

FAMILY-FRIENDLY TIP

Children and Boxer Grooming

Getting your kids into the act is an important tool for teaching them the responsibilities of pet ownership, and the Boxer makes it easy. During grooming, young children can hand you the supplies; older children can do the actual brushing. Save nail trims and general health checks for an adult, but show the kids that Boxer grooming can be a family affair.

wetness by shaking the water off his body. Rub him with a clean towel and keep him out of drafts until he's completely dry, and then watch the light gleam off that newly spruced coat.

Nail Care

Dogs in the wild never had to worry about trimming their toenails. Their daily treks in search of food kept nails worn down to a practical length. We can simulate this scenario with daily walks or runs on a hard surface. In fact, it's been said that if you have to trim your Boxer's nails, he's not getting enough exercise. This shouldn't be taken too literally; a Boxer can get plenty of good exercise in his fenced-in backyard, although the grass won't wear down his nails. But if you need motivation for regular runs or walks with your Boxer, nail trimming is as good as any.

Why is nail length important? If allowed to grow too long, toenails will interfere with the dog's natural walk. He'll tend to walk on the back of his feet, which can lead to splayed toes and an unattractive gait. In the extreme, excessively long toenails will curl under the feet and puncture toe pads. Long nails are also at risk of being snagged on a tree root or other obstacle, causing a painful toe injury.

On the topic of snagging nails, let's talk about dewclaws. Dewclaws are the nails by the fifth toe on each front *pastern,* the section of leg below the front knee joint and a prime location for snagging.

Dewclaws have been known to be torn off entirely, an extremely painful injury. If infection sets in, it can turn serious. To avoid this injury, most breeders have puppies' dewclaws surgically removed when they are still very young. By the time you brought your Boxer home, the dewclaw procedure was a distant memory.

How to Trim Your Boxer's Nails

Dogs generally don't like having their feet and toes handled, which can make nail trimming a challenge. Get them used to it from early puppyhood, and they won't give it a second thought. Start by fingering a puppy's paws and massaging his toes. Make the contact gentle and pleasant so that he will not only learn to accept it, he'll come to enjoy it. When he's comfortable having his feet handled, progress to snipping his nails.

Done properly, toenail trimming is painless, but accidents do happen, especially if the dog moves suddenly or the clippers slip and you accidentally cut the nail *quick,* the blood vessel at the bottom of the nail stem. The quick is easy to see if the Boxer has white toenails. If his nails are black, this area is more difficult to pinpoint. Shine a flashlight directly behind the nail; the quick will appear as a darker spot where the blood vessel

Done properly, toenail trimming is a painless procedure.

begins. You always want to trim *outside* the quick. If you go too short and cut the quick, your Boxer will let you know in no uncertain terms with a yelp. Err on the side of caution.

If you accidentally cut the quick, stop any bleeding with styptic powder, which is available at a drugstore. In a pinch, you can press the nail end into a soft bar of soap for a minute or two or apply cornstarch. Your stoic Boxer will forgive the rare accidental cut, but if it happens too often, he will head for the hills when you take out the clippers.

43

Ear Care

Whether or not your Boxer's ears are cropped, they will need regular attention to stay clean and healthy. Routine inspection of your dog's ears allows you to spot parasites, like ticks and ear mites, or any irritation and/or discharge that could be a sign of infection. Boxers who like to run through woods and underbrush need regular ear checks for burrs, cuts, and scratches.

How to Clean Your Boxer's Ears

For routine cleaning, dip a cotton ball in mineral oil. Hold the ear flap with one hand and gently wipe away any surface dirt, paying special attention to the nooks and crannies of the ear without poking down inside. Don't try to clean the inner ear with a cotton swab or anything else that might damage delicate tissues. Leave that to the vet, who has the equipment and expertise to safely examine the inner ear during routine checkups. If you think something is lodged in your Boxer's ear or he has an annoying wax buildup, don't attempt to remove it yourself and risk injury. Let a veterinary professional handle it.

Looking Good

Diagnosing Ear Problems

How do you know if your Boxer has an ear problem? His behavior is your best guide. If he frequently shakes his head, scratches his outer ear, or rubs the side of his head on the floor, take a look inside. Any redness and/or discharge means something is going on that requires medical attention. Yeast infections, a common side effect of antibiotic medication, produce an annoying itch and cottage-cheesy, malodorous discharge. The vet will probably prescribe medicated ear drops to ease discomfort and kill the fungus. To administer ear drops, hold the ear flap gently away from the head, and drop the recommended dosage into the ear canal. Release the flap and gently massage the outside of the entire ear to work the drops in.

If you decide to have your Boxer's ears cropped, you must be ready to commit to the necessary aftercare.

Ear Cropping

A common misconception is that ear cropping reduces a Boxer's chance of infections and other ear problems. This is not true. If anything, the natural ear flap can help protect the Boxer's inner ear from protruding branches and other day-to-day potential hazards. The practical reason for ear cropping—prevention of serious injuries during fighting and baiting—no longer exists in the mainstream world of Boxers.

The AKC Boxer breed standard requires ears to be cropped and standing upright to a tapering point, but if you don't plan to participate in conformation shows, ear cropping is a matter of choice. If you decide to have the surgery performed on your young Boxer, be ready to commit to the necessary aftercare and "training." (A splint is bound to the cropped ears to encourage them to stand upright.) It's best to find a vet who is experienced with the Boxer style, but there is no guarantee that cropped ears will stand up perfectly once they heal, possibly disqualifying the dog from conformation competition (dog showing).

The 1987 European Convention for the Protection of Pet Animals made ear cropping illegal in many countries. One day, the practice may be outlawed in the United States, but for now, American Boxer owners still have the option.

Eye Care

Routine eye care is a simple yet important part of your Boxer's health care regimen.

How to Clean Your Boxer's Eyes

A healthy dog will normally secrete clear mucus from his eyes, which you can easily wipe away with a soft tissue or damp cloth. Commercial products to remove "tear stains" (the narrow paths of mucus running down from the inner corners of the eyes) are available at pet supply stores and favored by dog show participants. If the discharge appears yellowish or bloody, consult your vet right away. Eye abnormalities should never be ignored.

SENIOR DOG TIP

Grooming the Older Boxer

The senior Boxer's slower lifestyle reduces his grooming needs but doesn't curtail them altogether. Toenails will still need trimming and in fact may become thicker and harder to cut. Regular body checks for tumors are important for the cancer-prone Boxer, especially as he ages. Help maintain the aging Boxer's appearance and well-being—and keep him feeling good—with a daily brushing and skin check.

How to Protect Your Boxer's Eyes

There are steps you can take at home to protect your Boxer's eyes. Make sure that his environment has no sharp objects at eye level. Outdoor environmental threats, like thorny plants and air pollution, are more difficult to control. You can't keep your Boxer in an airtight bubble, but you can do your best to keep him safe. Walk around the yard to

45

Looking Good

look for protruding twigs and branches, thorns, or sharp-leaved plants like holly. Check the fence; are there wood splinters or nails sticking out at his eye level?

If you live in an area where smog can be a problem, consider your Boxer's eyes as well as your own. If the air on a given day is not healthy for you, it's not good for your Boxer, either. If you are a smoker, be aware that a light breeze can waft an ash right into your Boxer's eye.

In a moving car, don't let your dog hold his head out of the open window. It's hard to deny him this pleasure—all those new smells just slapping him in the face!—but do it for safety's sake. Dirt and debris can come flying along with those tempting smells and could injure his eyes.

Dogs are also subject to many of the same eye conditions as humans are: sties, allergies, infections, and as they get older, cataracts. Regular eye exams by you and your vet will minimize any problems that may develop. You want your Boxer's expressive eyes to be clear and bright for a lifetime.

Dental Care

A dog's teeth are very strong—much sturdier than humans'—with a thick layer of enamel to protect against decay. They still require attention, however, and canine dental care has become much more proactive in recent years, resulting in healthier mouths for our dogs.

An oral health regimen is best started when your Boxer is a puppy, as he must learn to willingly accept your fingers or a toothbrush in his mouth without chomping on them. Puppy teeth are needle-sharp, and even when he outgrows them, you don't want your fingers in the mouth of an uncooperative adult Boxer.

How to Brush Your Boxer's Teeth

If your Boxer eats a diet of soft foods, he may develop tartar buildup on his teeth that makes his breath less than fresh and can lead to *gingivitis*, or gum disease. Keeping his mouth clean is easier than ever thanks to the many

Starting your puppy early on a regimen of oral care is the best way to promote a lifetime of cooperation.

Bad-Breath Remedies

If your Boxer has the bad-breath blues, first see the vet to make sure there is no underlying medical reason. If the cause is plain old halitosis, here are a few simple ways to make kissing him sweet:

- Buy a commercial breath freshener for dogs, usually chlorophyll drops or odor-neutralizing treats.
- Offer him a slice of apple or fresh parsley. Both have breath-freshening properties.
- Get serious about regular toothbrushing.

canine dental care products on the market with a dog's taste buds in mind. Toothpastes in dog-friendly flavors like chicken and beef make toothbrushing taste good. Never use human toothpaste, because it is not intended for consumption, and dogs don't know how to spit it out.

Starting your puppy early on a regimen of oral care is the best way to promote a lifetime of cooperation. He is more likely to accept your finger in his mouth, rather than a toothbrush, so begin by letting him sniff your finger, covered with a dental sheath. Pick a

time when your Boxer is tired and contented. If the sheath itself is unflavored, put a dab of dog toothpaste on it. As he licks it, slide it gently into his mouth, massaging gums and teeth. Practice this several times a week, and he will learn to accept toothbrushing as part of his routine.

If your Boxer's breath starts to wilt dandelions and there is no medical condition responsible, a professional teethcleaning may be in order to remove the plaque buildup. Even the placid Boxer won't sit still for a full dental exam and cleaning, so it must be done under general anesthesia. It's an easy procedure, but the inherent risks of anesthesia should always be considered. Your vet can help you decide if your Boxer's age or overall health presents added risk. Regular home dental care may not completely eliminate the need for a professional cleaning, but it will maximize its benefits.

With a healthy diet and regular checkups, your Boxer's pearly whites should last him a lifetime.

Good grooming is important, but it's no substitute for poor fitness or ill health. If a Boxer is not well cared for, all the brushing and nail trimming in the world won't hide it. The low-maintenance Boxer's best appearance is always presented in the shining eyes, happy smile, and energetic personality that come from responsible, loving care.

Chapter 5

Feeling Good

Your Boxer's good health depends on more than preventive veterinary medicine and your loving care. You must learn to interpret your Boxer's behavior and body language to identify possible health problems, as well as work as a team with your veterinarian to keep your pet hale and hearty.

Finding a Vet

How do you go about finding a veterinarian in the first place? The easiest way is to ask other dog owners in your area, preferably other Boxer owners. If you purchased you Boxer from a local breeder, she can give you a referral. Responsible breeders are picky about the professionals they entrust with their Boxers' welfare, so you can feel good about their choice. You are not obligated to use the same veterinarian as the breeder does, but there are advantages to doing so. Your Boxer's medical record will already be established,

Regular physical examinations play an important role in your Boxer's long-term health care plan.

since he's probably had his tail docked and first shots given by this vet. The Boxer breed and individual dog will be familiar to the vet. Another option is to contact the American Animal Hospital Association (AAHA) for a list of affiliated veterinarians in your area. You can also contact the nearest branch of your national breed club.

Ask the veterinary office staff when a good time would be for you to come by and tour their facility. They should be willing to show you around and discuss policies and procedures. Does the facility look clean and modern? Is the staff professional, compassionate, and competent? These are all good questions to ask, and a reputable animal hospital will have no problem answering them for you.

You want to be comfortable with the veterinarian caring for your dog, and vice versa. To really determine compatibility, make a get-acquainted appointment with the doctor you have chosen before any procedures need to be performed on your Boxer. It will be less stressful on the dog and will let you see how the vet interacts with him. Are you comfortable with the way she handles your Boxer? Does she allow sufficient time for your visit? Is she open to your questions and willing to explain things? If you like and trust your veterinarian, your Boxer will, too.

Annual Vet Visit

Regular physical examinations play an important role in your Boxer's long-term health care plan. It is usually during these exams that a vet picks up early warning signs of a serious issue that will affect the dog in the future. Early detection is your Boxer's best chance for correcting an acute problem or at least slowing its progress.

Nose

A cold, wet nose is not the legendary indicator of canine good health. Healthy Boxers' noses are often dry because their tongues don't always reach that high on the muzzle. Abnormal nasal discharge, however, could indicate distemper, a respiratory infection, or any number of diseases.

Eyes

Dull, lifeless eyes are the first sign that something is wrong. They can indicate stress, internal parasites, or a more serious illness. The vet will check for any debris or discharge, as contagious

FAMILY-FRIENDLY TIP

What to Tell Your Child About Vet Visits

A visit to the doctor—even a dog doctor—can be scary, but a child learning about responsible pet care should see the part a vet plays. Here are some tips to help:

- Explain that your Boxer needs checkups just like everyone in your family, especially since he can't tell you when something hurts.
- Remind the child that she'll see the vet do many of the same things the pediatrician does: look inside the ears, listen to the heart, look at the eyes, palpate the belly.
- Explain that the Boxer is not being hurt but that he may be nervous and quiet. Remember that a very young child may not understand the situation and can become emotional or fussy, agitating the dog and distracting the veterinarian.
- If your Boxer is receiving treatment for an illness, explain to the child what will be done and why. A child can process truthful information about the family pet more readily than if you avoid the subject entirely.

51

Feeling Good

Neutering

Neutering refers to the surgical removal of a dog's reproductive organs. For males, this means castration; for females, it means spaying, which is a partial or total hysterectomy. Neutering is the surest way to prevent indiscriminate mating that will result in unplanned, unwanted litters. It also keeps hormone levels down, so dogs are not inclined to roam and compete with other males for a mate. Spayed females are spared the potentially messy estrus reproductive phase, as well as certain diseases of the reproductive organs. Contrary to rumor, neutering does not turn an energetic dog into a lethargic couch potato, nor does the dog feel the loss of "manhood." It does ensure that one less dog contributes to the worldwide overpopulation of domestic animals.

eye infections often start with discharge from the eye corners.

Mouth

The mouth will be checked for lumps, cuts or scrapes, and the condition of the teeth. Healthy teeth should look clean and white; gums should be a deep pink. Lumps may indicate an abscessed tooth, oral

tumors, or an allergic reaction from an insect bite.

Ears

The vet will use an *otoscope,* a handheld instrument, to look inside these infamous bacteria harbors. She will also look for ear mites, highly transmittable parasites that can make your dog miserable. Discharge, foul smell, or inflammation can indicate infection.

Lungs

The vet will listen for any congestion or abnormal breathing patterns with a stethoscope. Chest congestion can indicate diseases like bordetella (kennel cough), distemper, and even heartworm.

Heart

A dog's normal heartbeat ranges from 100 to 130 beats per minute. Any abnormality is cause for concern. As with most diseases, early detection of heart disease is a dog's best chance for a longer, more comfortable life.

Skin and Coat

The skin is the largest organ in the body and reveals much about a dog's health. The vet will check the coat and skin for fleas, ticks, and other external parasites, as well as any swellings, abrasions, scaly patches, and lumps and the general coat condition. A healthy dog has a shiny, even coat.

Abdomen

The vet will palpate the dog's abdomen for lumps, abnormal distention, or possible infections. She will also pay attention to any signs of pain from the dog, which would indicate further problems.

Back and Tail

The vet will visually inspect and run her hand down the dog's spine and tail to check for any spinal problems like intervertebral disk disease, which is sometimes seen in Boxers.

Paws

The paws will be examined for any cuts or swelling.

Vaccinations

Long considered a crucial part of preventive veterinary medicine, vaccinations against diseases are sometimes required by law, as with rabies. This mandate protects your Boxer as much as other people. Anyone bitten by a dog lacking proof of rabies vaccination is considered at risk for the disease. And because a dog with early-stage rabies may be asymptomatic, the conclusive test must be done posthumously. Bluntly stated, if you ignore the rabies law, you risk your Boxer being put to sleep.

Rabies aside, the topic of vaccinations is controversial. Some dog owners believe that introducing toxins into the body does more harm than good. Other owners believe that if their dog spends minimal time outdoors, he doesn't have enough contact with the outside world to be at risk for disease. Assuming that responsible owners realize that Boxers shouldn't be exclusively "inside dogs," it's fair to say that Boxers benefit from vaccinations. Multiple-disease vaccines, such as the DHLPP combination that protects against distemper, hepatitis, leptospirosis, parvovirus, and parainfluenza are a practical and convenient way to give your Boxer an edge on longevity.

Even though relatively few preventable diseases are fatal, they can make your Boxer very uncomfortable or even permanently diminish his

53

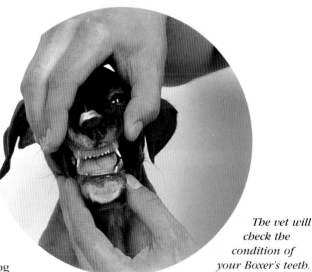

The vet will check the condition of your Boxer's teeth.

quality of life. Vaccinations against the following are the best way to keep your beautiful Boxer in the pink.

- **Canine bordetellosis,** also known as bordetella or kennel cough, is caused by a bacterium in the respiratory tract.
  Symptoms: Symptoms resemble a bad cold and include a runny nose and hacking cough.
  Treatment: Treatment includes isolating the dog to prevent the spread of infection and resting in a humid environment. Run a vaporizer or humidifier in his sleeping area, and encourage him to nap there. The illness should run its course in about two weeks.

- **Coronavirus** is an infection of the intestinal lining that is transmitted through feces and sometimes saliva.
  Symptoms: Lethargy, decreased appetite, and sudden diarrhea that is orange-tinted, malodorous, and possibly bloody.
  Treatment: May include IV fluids to combat dehydration and antibiotics to prevent secondary bacterial infections.

- **Distemper** is the number-one killer of unvaccinated dogs.
  Symptoms: Diarrhea, cough, anorexia, fever, nasal discharge, inflamed eyes, lethargy.
  Treatment: Treatment at the first sign of distemper greatly improves the dog's chances for recovery.

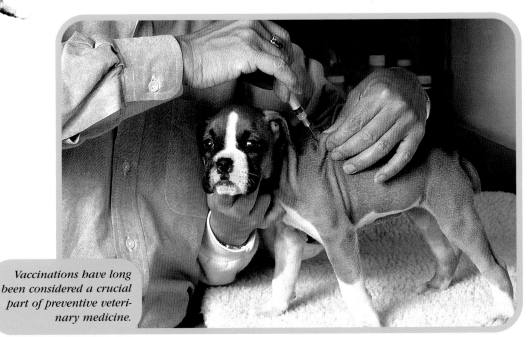

Vaccinations have long been considered a crucial part of preventive veterinary medicine.

Dogs with full-blown cases sometimes survive but are often left with permanent brain or nervous system damage.

- **Leptospirosis** is caused by a microorganism often carried by rats.
  Symptoms: Bloody stools or urine, fever, depression, red eyes and mouth, painful mouth sores, vomiting, thirst, anorexia, pain.
  Treatment: Quick treatment with antibiotics is necessary. Acute cases may require hospitalization.
- **Lyme disease** is a bacterium spread to dogs and humans through infected tick bites.
  Symptoms: Symptoms appear about two months after infection and include joint pain, fatigue, fever, and skin rash.
  Treatment: Treatment typically includes antibiotics and pain relievers. Recovery time depends on the severity of the case and how early it was detected.
- **Parainfluenza** is caused by several different viruses and a bacterium. It is not overtly dangerous but is highly contagious among dogs.
  Symptoms: Hacking cough.
  Treatment: Antibiotics to prevent complications and medicine to ease coughing.

Tick Removal

The simplest, safest way to remove a feeding tick is with a dedicated pair of blunt tweezers. Grasp the tick as close to the embedded head as possible, pull on it with steady pressure until it comes out, and flush it down the toilet. Try not to rupture or squeeze the tick's body so that potentially infectious body fluids don't get on your hand or the dog's skin. If the head is still attached to the dog after you have removed the tick, apply an antiseptic to the site. It will prevent infection, and the head will eventually fall off.

- **Parvovirus** was only discovered in dogs in 1977. It is believed to be a mutated strain of feline distemper.
  Symptoms: Depression and anorexia, followed by vomiting, diarrhea, and fever.
  Treatment: Treatment varies with the symptoms and severity of the disease, as well as the dog's age. Hospitalization is usually necessary. Your dog will probably receive medication to control vomiting and diarrhea, antibiotics to control secondary infections, and fluids to counteract dehydration.
- **Rabies** is transmitted by warm-blooded animals and is highly

contagious to humans and animals through infected saliva.

Symptoms: Change in disposition, pupil dilation leading to light intolerance, coordination difficulty, facial tics, random biting, loss of facial muscle control, coma.

Treatment: There is no effective treatment for this fatal disease, underscoring the importance of prevention.

Boxer-Specific Illnesses

Every dog breed has predispositions to certain medical conditions, and the Boxer is no exception. This doesn't mean that your Boxer is destined to develop one or more of those conditions or that he will escape any other type of medical problem. As with humans, a Boxer's genetic medical history can tell you what you should watch out for during your dog's lifetime and what may affect future generations.

Cardiomyopathy

One of the more serious diseases that can affect Boxers, *cardiomyopathy* is an inherited heart condition characterized by *arrhythmia*, or abnormal heart rhythm. It is a common cause of sudden death in Boxers of any age, often with no previous symptoms. The dog may have a seizure-like or fainting episode, or in the extreme, total heart failure. In some cases, the heart becomes enlarged, causing symptoms like shortness of breath, exercise intolerance, abdominal swelling, and coughing—the same as in humans with congestive heart failure. This is called *dilated*

A nutritious diet and plenty of exercise will help keep your Boxer healthy.

cardiomyopathy, and it occurs less frequently than cardiomyopathy with no heart enlargement.

There is no known cure for cardiomyopathy, and treatments vary in their effectiveness. To keep the disease from future Boxer generations, breeders look forward to the development of a definitive test for cardiomyopathy. Right now, the best tool for early detection is the Holter monitor, a 24-hour EKG that records heart activity and can detect arrhythmia in an asymptomatic dog with cardiomyopathy.

Aortic Stenosis

Another inherited heart defect plaguing Boxers is *aortic/subaortic stenosis (AS/SAS)*, a narrowing (*stenosis*) at or below (*subaortic*) the aortic heart valve. The heart must work harder to pump blood through the narrow vessel, and the heart muscle thickens over time. Afflicted dogs may display weakness or fainting, and some have been known to die abruptly. AS/SAS is usually detected after the discovery of of a *heart murmur*, a swishing sound made by the altered blood flow through the heart valve. Not all heart murmurs indicate AS/SAS, though, and a sonogram and/or echocardiogram can confirm or rule out the diagnosis.

There is no real treatment for AS/SAS beyond exercise restriction—a sad scenario for the typically energetic Boxer. Breeding is also out

Should You Insure Your Boxer?

This is a question to answer only after consideration of several factors. Boxers are not known as habitual biters, but any dog can potentially bite a human. Many homeowner's and renter's insurance policies cover injury from a dog bite; check what yours says. A dog who exhibits menacing behavior—not likely a Boxer—should have his own insurance coverage. Some breed-specific laws mandate it.

Pet health insurance is a boon to many Boxer owners, but it can be pricey and have restrictions. Does the policy limit your choice of veterinarian? Is your dog covered when he is traveling? Are certain breeds ineligible because they are deemed "vicious?" (The Boxer's ancestral linkage to pit-fighting dogs can haunt him even today.) Are the Boxer-specific health problems covered in the policy? What about preexisting conditions?

Do your homework, read the fine print, and then make an informed decision about insurance for your Boxer.

of the question for an AS/SAS-positive Boxer, who would pass the disease to his puppies.

Hip Dysplasia

Hip dysplasia is a painful, debilitating congenital disease manifested in a malformed hip joint. It is found in many dog breeds, including Boxers, and results from combined genetic and environmental factors. It almost always appears by the age of 18 months, and the effects range from mild stiffness to severe crippling. There is no real cure, although surgery can sometimes ease the symptoms. In extreme cases, a complete hip replacement will restore mobility

To help prevent bloat, try making your Boxer's mealtime as leisurely as possible.

and prevent recurrence, but it is an expensive proposition requiring a commitment to rehabilitation. Prevention is still the best medicine, and reputable Boxer breeders rely heavily on an x-ray test developed by the Orthopedic Foundation for Animals (OFA). This widely used test determines the absence or presence of hip dysplasia in a dog and should be required documentation on any

Boxer puppy you are thinking of buying. Both parents should have been tested and determined to be free of hip dysplasia.

Gastric Torsion (Bloat)

Technically known as *gastricdilation-volvulus syndrome* (GVD), *gastric torsion,* or *bloat,* is a swelling and twisting of a dog's stomach distended from gas, water, or both. When it occurs, the esophagus closes off, limiting the dog's ability to find relief by vomiting or belching. Sometimes the spleen becomes entrapped by the distended, twisted stomach, and blood supply is cut off. Shock and heart failure ultimately claim the dog's life. An otherwise healthy dog can die a painful death from bloat in a matter of hours. Only immediate veterinary care at its onset can save his life.

Deep-chested dog breeds like the Boxer have a predisposition to gastric torsion, but it is more often the result of gas taken in by the dog gulping food or water, especially after strenuous exercise. To prevent your Boxer from suffering this horrible condition, consider the following:

- Make mealtime as leisurely as possible. Place rubber chew toys in his food to discourage him from gulping his meal too fast.
- Serve two meals a day instead of just one to discourage ravenous gorging.
- Give him constant access to fresh water to prevent him from gulping large quantities at once.
- Wait one hour after meals before strenuous exercise, and wait one hour after exercise before feeding.
- Familiarize yourself with the symptoms of bloat. If it happens to your Boxer, you have literally only minutes to get help.

Symptoms of bloat include the following:

First-Aid Kit

A pet first-aid kit contains items you probably already have at home or can easily get at a drugstore. Keep it handy and well stocked to prevent expiration of medications and to ensure that you have what you need in an emergency:

- activated charcoal tablets
- adhesive tape (1 and 2 inches wide)
- antibacterial ointment (for skin *and* eyes)
- buffered or enteric-coated aspirin (*not* ibuprofen, which is toxic to dogs)
- cotton balls
- diarrhea medicine
- dosing syringe
- gauze pads
- hydrogen peroxide (3%)
- petroleum jelly
- rectal thermometer
- rubber gloves
- rubbing alcohol
- scissors
- tourniquet
- towels
- tweezers

- Restlessness, uneasiness, or inability to lie down comfortably
- Repeated futile attempts to vomit
- Drooling
- Rapid, shallow breathing
- Very pale, very red, or blue gums
- Distended, bloated abdomen
- Dazed look, as if in shock

If your Boxer exhibits any of these symptoms, seek immediate help, and don't panic. Call ahead so the vet can prepare for your arrival. She will first try to decompress the stomach with a stomach tube. If this doesn't remedy the situation, immediate surgery will be necessary to correct the twisted stomach, remove unhealthy tissue, and anchor the stomach in place (called *gastroplexy*) to avoid recurrence of bloat.

Thyroid Disease

In the Boxer, thyroid disease is usually manifested in *hypothyroidism*, or low thyroid hormone (T4) levels. It often develops

Have your veterinarian examine any masses or unusual lumps on your Boxer.

slowly over months or years for unknown reasons. Symptoms include listlessness, coarse hair, significant hair loss, weight gain, neurological problems, and infertility.

Unfortunately, the blood test for hypothyroidism is often inaccurate. A symptomatic dog can yield a normal result on the simple T4 test. A dog who continues to be symptomatic after normal T4 results could benefit from a comprehensive panel of tests.

Treatment for hypothyroidism is lifelong but simple: a hormone supplement taken once or twice daily.

Cancer

Cancer can and does occur in all dog breeds at all ages, but it seems to be a particular bane of Boxers. *Lymphosarcoma* or *lymphoma* (cancer of the lymph system), *mast cell tumors* (cancer of the specialized cells that help the dog respond to inflammation and allergies), and *squamous cell carcinomas* (cancerous skin lesions) are among the most common forms diagnosed. Owners should closely monitor their Boxers for any masses or unusual lumps. Beyond a healthy lifestyle and regular medical checkups, there is nothing specific you can do to prevent cancer. The earlier it is diagnosed, the greater the chances for successful treatment.

General Illnesses

Every dog, regardless of breed, will probably experience some kind of general illness in his lifetime. It helps to know some of the more common conditions that can befall your Boxer and how to handle them.

Parasites

Parasites fall into two categories: internal and external. Both can be the bane of your Boxer's existence if not treated. They can make him uncomfortable and sick, and in extreme cases, they can kill.

Internal Parasites

A dog with intestinal worms will show signs of general malaise: a dry coat, dull eyes, lethargy, vomiting, diarrhea, and weight loss despite a hearty appetite. Some dogs may lose their appetite entirely, and still others will be asymptomatic until worm infestation makes them severely anemic. Because all kinds of worms produce similar symptoms, the dog's stools must be tested to determine

Hyperplasia

Boxers are predisposed to an overgrowth of gum tissue, or hyperplasia. The overgrown tissues are not painful or harmful, but they cause other problems. They can grow to a point where a tooth crown is buried under the overgrown tissue and the tooth becomes useless. Overgrown tissues also form pockets that are the perfect breeding ground for bacteria. Fortunately, the overgrowths can be snipped off while the dog is under general anesthesia. Recovery is quick and virtually painless.

exactly what parasite he's dealing with.

- **Heartworms**: Heartworms are deadly parasites transmitted from dog to dog through mosquito bites. It can take a full eight months after the bite for the worms to mature and settle in the heart vessels. Symptoms include chronic cough, weight loss, and fatigue. Heart failure ultimately claims the dog's life.
  Heartworm infestation is treatable,

but therapy is expensive, long, and risky, though not as dangerous as the heartworms themselves. The process kills the adult heartworms, but dead worms in the heart can provoke a fatal clot in the blood vessels or chambers. Prevention is a far better option. Your vet can tell you the right age to start your dog on a heartworm preventive. It is crucial that your dog be tested and found heartworm-free before starting a preventive regimen. A dog already harboring heartworms can become critically ill from the same medicine that prevents infestation. Prevention is not foolproof, and there is always a slight chance that your dog can become infested after taking the preventive. Because the symptoms do not present themselves for many months, you could innocently make your infected dog sick by continuing his heartworm preventive. Yearly blood tests for heartworms should be part of every dog's health care routine.

• **Hookworms:** In dogs, hookworms attach themselves to the intestines to feed, changing locations about six times a day. Because a dog loses blood each time the hookworm repositions itself, the dog can become anemic. Symptoms of hookworm infestation include dark stools, weight loss, general weakness, pale skin coloration, and skin that is swollen and red from penetration of the larvae, usually at the feet. Fortunately, there are a number of proven medications to rid the host of these parasites. Most heartworm preventives include a hookworm insecticide, as well.

• **Ringworm:** Ringworm is not really a worm but a very contagious fungus that spreads easily among animals and humans through contact with infected skin or hair.

Infective spores are constantly dropped off the hair and skin of infected dogs or people, and contact with even one spore is all it takes to catch it. Ringworm feeds on dead surface skin and hair cells, causing an irritating itch. It typically appears on dogs as a raw-looking or scaly bald patch.

Ringworm is difficult to eliminate, as it is hardy and can live for years in the environment. Treatment is a combination of topical and systemic therapy, but ringworm can be resistant. Painstaking attention to hygiene and complete decontamination of the dog's environment must be continued until the vet declares the dog ringworm-free.

- **Roundworms:** Common parasites in puppies as well as adult dogs, roundworms look like strands of spaghetti and feed on the host's digesting food. The condition is easily treated, but humans in the family who have contact with a puppy infested with roundworms

A little knowledge goes a long way toward disease prevention.

Common Internal Parasites

The following are some common internal parasites that you should be on the lookout for in your Boxer:

- heartworms
- hookworms
- ringworm
- roundworms
- tapeworms
- whipworms

must be especially vigilant about their own hygiene. If a stool sample confirms the presence of roundworms, there are a variety of effective drugs your vet may prescribe. Over the course of treatment, stool samples will be checked for efficacy.

- **Tapeworms:** The tapeworm is actually a parasite of a parasite, entering a dog's system via bites from fleas carrying tapeworm eggs. The larvae move into the intestines, where they develop into adults, sometimes growing to be several feet (m) long. Adult tapeworms feed on the host's digesting food, robbing him of nutrition. Extreme cases can be fatal.

  Dogs infected with tapeworms rarely exhibit symptoms, and the worms don't always appear in a dog's stools. Detection comes when small segments of worm appear around the anus, resembling wriggling grains of rice. Treatment is with a solution administered orally or by injection, but you also need to address the issue of fleas, as they are the most common tapeworm carriers.

- **Whipworms:** In North America, whipworms are among the most common parasitic worms in dogs. These worms attach themselves to the lower part of the intestine to feed and can live for months or even years in a dog, causing anemia. Dogs can ingest eggs or immature worms by eating infected animal feces, a habit that can be as harmful as it is distasteful.

  Whipworms can be difficult to diagnose. The only way to detect them is with a stool sample, and even this is not infallible. Dogs successfully treated with deworming agents are often reinfected from exposure to the eggs deposited on the ground in the feces. Whipworm eggs can survive in the elements for as long as five years, waiting to infest or reinfest a host. This emphasizes the importance of cleaning up droppings, whether in your own backyard or a public park.

External Parasites

These buggers all think your Boxer would make the perfect host, but guests like these will only make him uncomfortable and potentially sick. They can be found anywhere on his body but typically settle down on the head and neck.

- **Fleas:** Fleas are by far the hardest external parasite to eliminate. Not only do they reproduce incredibly fast, but they also can actually adapt to insecticides and become resistant. To check for the presence of fleas, separate a patch of your Boxer's fur to examine his skin. If you see tiny black flecks resembling pepper, that's flea dirt, or excrement. You will undoubtedly find your dog scratching a lot, as well. Some dogs develop serious allergic reactions to fleabites, which makes them miserable. Prompt veterinary treatment is in order to ease the skin irritations and prevent infection. Your vet will also tell you how to rid the dog and your home of these stubborn pests.
- **Mites:** Ear mites irritate your Boxer's sensitive ears and produce a dry, rusty-brown discharge. If you see your dog constantly scratching or pawing at his ears, or you notice inflammation or discharge, have your vet check for ear mites.

Mange mites are tiny critters that can cause big dermatological problems for your Boxer in the form of sarcoptic mange, making his skin itchy and crusty and raising little red bumps. Follicular mange is caused by a different type of mite and may or may not cause itching, but it will cause small, bare patches in your dog's fur. Medicine from the vet will clear up this condition.

- **Ticks:** Ticks burrow their mouths into the skin to feed on the host's blood. They are infamous disease-carriers of such illnesses as Lyme disease and Rocky Mountain spotted fever. As discussed earlier, the simplest, safest way to remove a tick is to pull it out with a dedicated pair of blunt tweezers. Grasp the tick as close to its head as possible, pull on it with steady pressure until it comes out, and

65

Examine your Boxer for ticks after he has been playing outside.

flush it down the toilet. Try not to rupture or squeeze the tick's body to prevent potentially infectious body fluids from making contact with your hand or your dog's skin. If part of the tick's head remains attached to the dog, apply an antiseptic to the site. The head will eventually fall off.

Allergies

Grouped into four categories, allergies can be as bothersome to our dogs as they are to us. They are manageable, though, with help from your vet.

Flea Allergy

The most common type of allergy seen in dogs, flea allergy isn't brought on by the flea itself but by a protein in its saliva that's left in the dog's skin after a fleabite. Severe reactions can make the dog miserable. Your vet can advise you on how to soothe the dog's skin and how to get rid of the fleas.

Inhalant or Atopic Allergy

Inhalant allergies are the second most common type of allergy in dogs, who experience them when they breathe in the offending allergen, whether it is pollen, tobacco smoke, or mold spores. Outside allergens will find their way into your house and your dog's nose, so keeping your dog indoors doesn't always help. Your vet can discuss treatment with you.

Food Allergy

Food allergies in dogs are often caused by some of the same foods that humans are allergic to: soy, milk, eggs, wheat, corn, and chicken. The most likely reaction is itchy, irritated skin, although vomiting and diarrhea may occur. The offending food must be isolated by trial and error and eliminated from the dog's diet.

Contact Allergy

Contact allergy reactions occur from physically touching a substance (such as plastic, grass, or wool) containing an allergen. Allergy shots are often used to cope with the uncomfortable symptoms, and lifestyle changes may be necessary. A Boxer who is allergic to his plastic food dish, for example, should be switched to a steel or ceramic bowl. The owner of a Boxer who is allergic to grass must provide an alternate surface for exercise and relaxation, such as an enclosed tennis court to run in or an asphalt or cement path, sidewalk, or road for long, brisk walks, and a dog bed for the backyard.

Allergies cannot be genetically controlled or predicted, but they can be managed. It takes patience and tenacity to identify the problem, as well as determination to work around it.

Allergies are manageable with help from your vet.

Eye Conditions

Dogs are subject to many of the eye conditions humans are, plus a few extra that pertain to the specific canine eye structure. Genetics can play a part in a dog's eye health, so before buying any puppy, ask the breeder about certification of parental eye health from the Canine Eye Registration Foundation (CERF). Certain eye conditions, such as those described below, are commonly seen in Boxers.

Cherry Eye

In this condition, the gland of the third eyelid, which produces about one-third of the dog's total tear film, protrudes (*prolapses*) over the rim of the lid. The resulting pink, fleshy mass can become inflamed and ulcerated. Surgery can restore the gland to its normal position.

Corneal Dystrophy

In this disease, one or more parts of the cornea (the clear surface that covers the front of the eye) lose clarity due to a buildup of cloudy material. In some cases, painful ulcerations will form, while in others, the dog experiences no bothersome symptoms. The condition is strictly inherited; outside factors, such as injury or diet, play no part in its presentation. Treatment is usually pain medication, or in extreme cases, surgery.

Progressive Retinal Atrophy (PRA)

This genetic disease causes the retina of the eye to degenerate. An afflicted dog will first experience night blindness, followed by loss of daytime vision. There is no way to prevent the

Feeling Good

inevitable blindness, but some vets have found that nutritional therapy can delay it. Most dogs adapt well to blindness, so although the condition is heartbreaking for owners, Boxers with PRA can still enjoy a good quality of life.

Ear Conditions

In a healthy Boxer, ear care is usually low maintenance. The inside skin of the outer ear should be clean, pink, and smooth. If there is an ear problem, your Boxer will tell you by frequently shaking his head or pawing at his ear. Take a look. Is there irritation and redness? Is there a discharge and/or odor? If so, a trip to the vet is in order.

An old wives' tale says that cropped ears are less prone to infection than uncropped ears are. While some breeds with pendulous ears, like the Basset Hound, may be prone to infections because of the continually

warm, moist environment inside the ear, the natural ear of the Boxer allows plenty of air circulation and, in fact, helps protect the inner ear from dirt, debris, and other hazards.

Aural Hematomas

An aural hematoma is a swelling of the earflap, a fairly common problem seen in all breeds, most often in retrievers. Blood vessels in the ear rupture, causing the space between the skin and the cartilage to fill with blood or serum. The cause is unclear (as with human nosebleeds), though often there are underlying reasons (ear mites, porcupine quills, or allergies) that account for the excess pressure and inflammation.

Left untreated, the ear will become painful, and scarring will occur. Medical treatments do not always work, but you should try them before resorting to surgical correction. Your vet can prescribe medications to ease the pain and make your pet more comfortable.

Ear Mites

The most common ear disorder in dogs, these parasites usually affect the outer ear canal, although other parts of the ear can be affected, too. They cause itching and

If your Boxer's ear are manifesting any irritation, redness, discharge, or an odor, take him to the veterinarian immediately.

irritation, prompting the dog to shake his head and scratch his ears, worsening the irritation. Ear mites will leave dark brown droppings in the outer ear, coupled with a foul smell. Your vet will prescribe a monthlong treatment to flush out the ears and kill any eggs.

Yeast Infections

Yeast organisms are rarely the main cause of ear infections, but they have a way of invading moist or irritated ears, prime real estate for proliferation. Yeast inflammation is often a side effect of antibiotics, affecting ears and/or toes and usually easy to identify: a thick, whitish discharge and a yeasty smell.

Yeast infections cause intense itching and irritation. The vet will prescribe medicine that takes care of both uncomfortable symptoms.

Alternative Therapies

Over the past few decades, alternative approaches to animal health care have surfaced as companions to the science of veterinary medicine. *Alternative*, or *holistic*, medicine purports that illness and wellness result from combined emotional and physical factors and advocates natural remedies, usually ingredients found in plants. This theory, along with ancient disciplines like *reiki* and *acupuncture*, has found its way into modern veterinary care. Holistic vets can be hard to find, but this may change as more veterinarians branch out into

What Is a Holistic Veterinarian?

A holistic veterinarian believes that optimal health and well-being are achieved through preventive medicine and supporting the animal's own healing process. Holistic vets are usually trained in one or more therapies, such as chiropractic, acupuncture, or homeopathy, and they pay particular attention to diet and nutrition. They also regard animals as emotional and spiritual beings, a perspective shared by many dog owners.

This doesn't mean that a vet who doesn't call himself holistic isn't devoted to helping animals. What matters is that your vet is willing to explore new ideas in health care or at least discuss them with you.

alternative health care. A balance between alternative remedies and scientific medicine is the best road to a long and healthy life for your Boxer.

Acupuncture

Literally translated as "needle piercing," acupuncture involves inserting very fine needles into the skin to stimulate specific anatomic points in the body for healing purposes. Practiced for centuries by the Chinese, acupuncture is regarded by Western cultures as a complement to traditional medicine. Holistic veterinarians practice this painless procedure on dogs for a variety of health issues.

Reiki

Reiki (Japanese for "universal life force") is a hands-on healing technique that seeks to rebalance blocked life-force energy. Useful for pain relief, promoting natural healing, and restoring emotional well-being, the emphasis is on transmission of

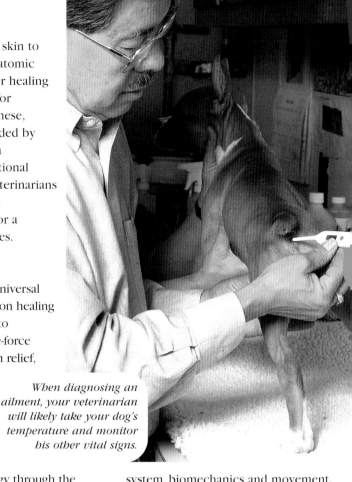

When diagnosing an ailment, your veterinarian will likely take your dog's temperature and monitor his other vital signs.

information and energy through the practitioner's touch. Many dog owners claim that reiki healed their pet when nothing else did, but there is no scientific proof. If you are open to the idea of spiritual healing methods, reiki doesn't interfere with traditional medical treatments and may help your dog.

Chiropractic

Chiropractic (Greek for "hand practice") is based on the relationship of the spinal column to the nervous

system, biomechanics and movement, and the circulatory system. Chiropractors manipulate the vertebrae to relieve many joint, nerve, and muscle problems and to alter disease progression. The same principles that bring relief to human patients can help dogs as well.

Homeopathy

Based on the principle that "like cures like," homeopathic remedies are made of diluted amounts of the same substance that caused the symptoms in the first place. The theory is that the original substance in a highly diluted form stimulates the patient's life force to begin healing. For example, ipecac syrup is used to induce vomiting. In a homeopathic remedy for vomiting, ipecac in very small amounts can relieve vomiting. Veterinary homeopathy can be practiced in conjunction with conventional medical treatment.

Herbal Therapy

Humans have used herbs for their curative properties since time immemorial, and the restorative effects are safe for dogs, too. Be sure to consult your vet before embarking on any alternative treatment, herbal or otherwise. Drug interactions, allergic reactions, and herbal product quality are important considerations that you should explore together.

Companion animals are a lifelong commitment, not a passing fancy, and we owe them the best possible life for their whole life. Good health is a gift, to us as well as to our pets. We need to show our appreciation for this gift by taking care of ourselves and the dogs who rely on us for everything. With good food, plenty of exercise, a lot of love, and regular veterinary care, our Boxers will continue to enrich our lives for many happy years.

SENIOR DOG TIP

The Silver Boxer and Declining Health

A Boxer becomes a "senior citizen" at seven, even though you may not see any decrease in his energy level or appetite. At some point, though, his fur will turn silver, he will sleep a little more, and he will play a little less vigorously and for a shorter time period. His teeth and gums may need extra care, and his hearing and/or sight may deteriorate. In short, older dogs experience many of the same physical changes as aging humans do—they just cope with them better!

You can help your aging Boxer with ramps to help him climb up to your bed and with dog food specially formulated for seniors, but sometimes old-age infirmities require lifestyle adaptations. You may need to visually alert a deaf Boxer to your presence. A partially paralyzed Boxer will need a canine wheelchair to get around. An incontinent Boxer means extra cleanups and possibly diapers. But remember, you signed on for the long haul. With extra love and extra effort, you can help your silver Boxer make the most of his golden years.

Feeling Good

Chapter 6

Being Good

Responsible dog ownership includes keeping control of your dog at all times. The average Boxer is about 55 pounds (24.5 kg) of exuberance that can accidentally topple a small child or even an unsteady adult. At best, an ill-mannered Boxer will not be welcome in very many places. At worst, a Boxer-related incident will cost you time and money.

Why Train Your Boxer?

Family dogs who know their boundaries feel happier and more secure. They are creatures of habit who thrive when they know what to expect and what is expected of them. Too many pets go untrained because owners equate obedience training to boot camp—physically harsh and emotionally stressful. Training isn't about breaking your Boxer's spirit; it's about helping him reach his potential. Pack animals find security in knowing their place in the scheme of things, and working breeds like Boxers shine when they have "jobs" to do: agility, conformation, therapy work, or simply obeying their humans' simple commands.

The Power of Positive Training

As anyone who has ever toilet trained a toddler knows, compliance is best achieved through *positive* reinforcement, which means that rewards come when the "trainee" does what you want, rather than punishing him when he doesn't. Where is the incentive to please you if all you do is punish the dog for something he doesn't understand? The smart Boxer quickly figures out what you want from him and will readily comply if the action culminates in praise, affection, or in the beginning, treats.

Positive training is more than bending the Boxer to your will or bribing him to perform tricks. A Boxer must be trained to choose to obey you of his own accord. The intelligence and independent thinking that make your Boxer so trainable can also tempt him to disobey you. If he chooses to ignore your *stay* command in favor of a squirrel chase, though, you may lose more than your pride. You may lose your Boxer to an accident. Fortunately, ongoing training will give

Praise and treats are great ways to positively reinforce your Boxer for a job well done.

your Boxer a sense of achievement, help you bond with him in a special way, and help keep him safe.

Socialization

Socialization means exposing your Boxer to every kind of ordinary situation he may encounter during his lifetime: large crowds, rowdy children, the disabled, different environments, loud noises, and other animals. The socialization he receives up to the age of three months will largely determine the impressions he develops about the outside world. A lack of socialization during puppyhood can manifest as a fearful or aggressive older dog. Socialization begins while a puppy is still in his breeder's care, and it is up to you to continue this all-important process. It is one of the best things you will do for your Boxer.

Socializing the Boxer Puppy

Boxers can be dog-aggressive by nature, underscoring the importance of socialization as early in life as possible. For the first three months of life, a puppy develops lifelong impressions about the outside world. Take your debutante Boxer out with you whenever possible to the park, to pet-

The Expert Knows

Finding a Trainer

Finding the right trainer to work with both you and your Boxer is as important as the training itself. She should suit your personality, your dog's personality, and your philosophy on dog handling. A good trainer is fair, consistent, immediate, and appropriate in discipline. Affection should color every aspect of training, even reprimands. Ask around for trainer referrals, and then observe a few at work. Do you like the way the trainer handles the dogs in class? Do the dogs seem comfortable with this trainer? Would you be comfortable putting your Boxer in this trainer's hands? Talk to the human students. Are they satisfied with the results they see in their dogs? With a little research, you can find an affordable, knowledgeable trainer to bring out the best in your Boxer.

friendly stores, on a walk downtown, or to any safe place you normally visit during everyday life. Remember, though, that the world as a whole is still relatively new to your little Boxer. Loud noises, large vehicles, and bright flashing lights can frighten him. Leave him in the security of his crate at home if you are attending a fireworks display or demolition derby. Even well-socialized adult dogs can become anxious at those kinds of events.

Boxers should be exposed to all kinds of people in all kinds of

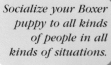

Socialize your Boxer puppy to all kinds of people in all kinds of situations.

situations, as well as other animals. Introduce him to neighborhood pets, under your watchful eye, of course. Familiarize him with people of various races, ages, and genders, as well as people in wheelchairs, on crutches, and using canes or walkers.

A lack of puppyhood socialization can result in a fearful or aggressive adult dog. Besides, socializing gives you a chance to show off your

Boxer puppy, and he gets to enjoy extra attention.

Socializing the Adult Boxer

What about the adult Boxer who is adopted or rescued from an abusive situation? The good news is that dogs of any age can benefit from obedience classes that focus on positive reinforcement. Even a shy dog who mistrusts everyone—*especially* a shy

where he can sleep, relax, and travel in security. A "freedom fantasy" has poisoned many people against the idea of crate training, denouncing it as cruel and unnatural to social animals. Actually, a dog's denning instinct makes crate training a breeze. Most dogs enjoy their crate, as long as it is a place of refuge, not punishment. It ensures a puppy's safety when you are unable to supervise him. Crate training is not cruel—it is the responsible thing to do.

Benefits of Crate Training

A puppy's instinct not to soil his living space plays a big part in housetraining, and the crate accelerates this process. The limited crate space encourages a puppy to "hold it" until he is removed to an appropriate elimination spot. Remember the limitations of a young puppy's bladder and bowel control, and don't leave him inside his crate more than a couple of hours at a time.

How to Crate Train

Despite the denning instinct, it may take a puppy some time to appreciate the crate as his own special place. He won't be happy at first about being isolated, so introduce him to the crate before you actually need to confine him in it. Line the crate with thick layers of newspaper that make a more comfortable surface and absorb accidents. Prop open the crate door and toss a treat inside, saying, "Crate." Allow him to go inside for the treat,

dog who mistrusts everyone—can learn to trust humans and develop self-confidence. A timid rescued Boxer needs help to conquer his fears and prevent fear biting. Compassionate, patient reconditioning can make him a happier, safer dog.

Crate Training

Crate training is not imprisonment; it is familiarizing your Boxer to a haven

sniff around a bit, and come out when he's ready. Leave the door open for him to come and go as he pleases.

When your dog seems comfortable with the crate, serve his next meal inside with the door open. When he is comfortable with that, start closing the crate door during meals. When he is finished, take him immediately outside to relieve himself. Very soon, he will regard the crate not as a prison but as a cozy spot where good things occur. At naptime during the day, put him in his crate and shut the door, teaching him that the crate is also a nice place to snooze.

At bedtime, put the crate close to your bed, where your Boxer can sense your proximity. A puppy will probably cry the first night or two, but resist the temptation to let him out. When he whines, say, "Quiet" firmly, or lightly tap your hand on top of the crate. You want him to know that he may come out only when he is quiet and you are ready, not when he has a tantrum. If the crying persists in the middle of the night, your Boxer probably needs to eliminate. Take him outside, praise him when he eliminates, and then put him back into the crate and say goodnight.

Housetraining

With a new puppy, the first order of business is to teach him where to do his business. Housetraining begins right away, but don't expect too much at first. The learning curve varies from dog to dog, and your Boxer's elimination control is limited, so be patient.

How to Housetrain

Before you bring your Boxer home, prepare for housetraining by collecting in a sealable plastic bag some urine-soaked litter from the puppy's living area at his breeder's. Scatter it around the outdoor area at your house where you want him to relieve himself. The scent will identify this site as the appropriate place to go. Take him there directly upon

Treats

Treats play a big role in your Boxer's life. They should never take the place of a balanced meal, but for rewards, treats are hard to beat. For training, bite-size, meaty treats like pieces of hot dog work best. Commercial treats with wholesome ingredients and no chemical additives are good, albeit more expensive, choices. Don't overlook your pantry: Foods like plain rice cakes, peanut butter, sliced apple, or carrots make satisfying, low-calorie Boxer treats. To avoid giving him a snack that may make him sick, check with your vet before experimenting. Chocolate, onions, and macadamia nuts, for example, are toxic to dogs.

arriving home and wait until he eliminates. This may take some time, so be patient. When he goes, make him think that he has just performed a feat of Olympic proportions and you couldn't be more pleased.

During your puppy's first few months with you, watch for telltale signs that he needs to eliminate. If he walks around, sniffing the floor, he's searching for the scent that tells him it's the right place to go. Take him there right away and praise him when he functions. Always take him outside right after eating, drinking, or sleeping, lavishing praise on him when he goes in the right spot.

If Your Boxer Has an Accident

Accidents are a fact of life during housetraining, but your reaction affects his progress. Never punish your Boxer by striking him or rubbing his nose in his mistake. He'll understand your displeasure, but he'll connect it with elimination itself, not with eliminating in the wrong place. This mixed message can diminish his trust in you and make training more difficult.

If you catch your puppy in the act of eliminating, take him immediately to where he should finish the job. He may be distracted by the interruption and need a few extra minutes. When he is done, praise him generously to show your approval of *this* site.

If you discover a mistake in the house after the fact, it's too late for damage control. He won't connect your disapproval with something he did even a few minutes ago. Resolve to keep a sharper eye on him, and clean up the mess immediately with a product that neutralizes waste

79

Most dogs enjoy their crates, as long as they are a place of refuge, not punishment.

Boxer Body Language

A Boxer's eyes may speak volumes, but so does his body language. Frequent use of front paws in play and skirmishes contributed to the breed's name. In addition, every Boxer lover knows about the unique "Boxer Bend": the C-shape that Boxers curl their bodies into when pleased or excited.

Dogs also use their ears, eyes, tail, and voice to communicate. Here are a few examples of common canine comments:

Body Language	What It Means
Dog looks at you sideways with a lowered head.	"I'm worried and unsure of your next move."
Dog stares at you with an elevated head, standing on tiptoes.	"I'm equal to the challenge and ready to pounce."
Front half of dog's torso is lowered in a bow.	"Let's play!"
Dog's entire body is crouched, with tail hanging down and ears folding back.	"I submit to you."
Dog's lips are curled back and fangs are exposed.	"Watch out!"
Fur down the center of dog's back is standing on end.	"I'm afraid but ready to defend myself."

scents. Ordinary home cleaners kill germs but do nothing to remove the scent that now identifies your carpet as an elimination site.

Remember that an accident in the house is not your Boxer's fault—it's yours. Somewhere along the line, your supervision lapsed, even for a brief minute or two. Don't scold him for your oversight. If you cannot watch him closely, take him outside to eliminate, and then crate him for a while. He isn't likely to soil there. With patience and consistency,

your Boxer will be housetrained in short order.

Basic Obedience Commands

The crucial time for a puppy to learn basic obedience is in his first few weeks at home. Because of puppies' limited attention spans, training sessions should be only about ten minutes. Repetition is the key, as puppies have short memories. It's more effective to go through several brief sessions throughout the day instead of one marathon.

Whether he will be a polite therapy dog or an agility competitor, the first commands any dog should learn are *sit, come, stay, down,* and *heel* (walk nicely on a leash). These Basic Five not only make your Boxer delightful to be with, but they also ensure his safety. Your command to stay when he wants to take off after something in traffic, for example, may be the only thing preventing him from being hit by a car. The Boxer's quick intelligence promises rapid mastering of these simple commands.

Sit

This command is invariably the first one a dog learns, and with good reason. It is something he already knows how to do. The trick is to get him to do it when *you* want him to. Every training session should begin and end with a *sit*, so that even if your Boxer doesn't readily pick up the next command,

The sit *command is commonly one of the first commands a dog will learn.*

you'll inspire confidence by ending the session on a positive, treat-filled note.

How to Teach Sit

To teach the *sit* command, put a training collar and leash on your Boxer, and hold the leash in your left hand. Hold a treat in your right hand by his nose, and let him sniff and lick the treat but not take it. He now has incentive. Slowly raise your treat hand from in front of his nose to upward over his head. His eyes will follow, and he will naturally assume a seated position. Say, "Sit" at the exact moment his head goes up and his rear goes down. Immediately give him the treat and lots of praise.

Come

Puppies learn this command easily, but it is more challenging for adult dogs to maintain. Most puppies will gladly approach you, summoned or not. But by the time they reach doggy adolescence, which is around six months, the siren call of a squirrel or some tantalizing odor may supersede your command. It is easy to teach *come*, but if misapplied, the command can be easily unlearned. Therefore, you should *never*

Being Good

FAMILY-FRIENDLY TIP

How to Involve Your Child in Boxer Training

Dog training is truly a family affair, so the whole family should be on board with it. Older children should accompany you to obedience class to see what they need to practice at home. You can also use training as an opportunity to teach younger children that animals should always be treated with loving kindness. Let children know that their roles in the family Boxer's training are just as important as those of the adults. Practice simple commands with the kids so that your Boxer can train even when you can't. You will appreciate the extra help!

call your Boxer to come and then punish him. Any negative association with the command unravels all training progress in an instant. You should also refrain from using the command too frequently or your Boxer will be tempted to ignore you. It is better to spring an unexpected "Come!" when he is distracted by play or something else. You want him to learn to heed your call no matter what else is going on.

How to Teach Come

To teach this command, kneel down and hold your arms wide, saying, "Come!" You shouldn't even need a treat to entice him, but he does need to learn that the *come* command doesn't mean that he should bowl you over. When he's about 3 feet (0.9 m) away from impact, say, "Sit" with a treat in your outstretched hand. When he stops to investigate the treat, put him into a *sit* and praise him. Repeat the exercise.

Heel

Heeling occurs when a dog matches his pace to that of the human walking him. It is an important command for the powerful Boxer to learn, or else he'll end up walking you.

How to Teach Heel

Preheeling begins when the puppy learns to follow you off lead. Young puppies will naturally follow you, their pack leader. Cash in on this by saying, "Come" to reinforce the action while he's doing it. Alternatively, you can squat down, hold your arms wide, and say, "Come," an invitation no Boxer puppy can resist.

When he is ready to move on to leash walking, put him in a *sit* next to your left foot with the leash in your left hand. Say, "Heel," and step off with your left foot. If he doesn't move when you do, slap the coils of excess leash against your leg to urge him to step off. Walk together about three steps, stop, and tell him, "Sit." When he does so, praise him and then repeat the *heel*. Keep praising him as long as he stays by your left leg while walking three steps. If he veers away or stops, put him into a *sit* and start over. Once he has mastered heeling for three steps, increase it to five, and so on. Before long, he'll be heeling like a pro.

Stay

Teaching *stay* to a puppy who wants to be with you every moment is a challenge, because you're also teaching him to walk at your side with the *heel* command. How do you now teach him that he must stay at some distance from you?

How to Teach Stay

To teach *stay*, put him into a sit next to your left leg. Place your right hand (concealing a treat) at his nose, and say, "Stay" with a "stop" gesture in front of his face. Step forward with your right foot and stand in front of him, relaxing the leash's tautness. Let him lick the treat in your hand (but not take it) while you count to five, and then turn back to the heel position. If he stayed for those few seconds, he has earned a treat. If he stepped out of position when you moved away,

Teaching your Boxer to walk nicely on leash is an essential obedience lesson.

Training the Older Dog

Anyone who thinks you can't teach an old dog new tricks obviously never had a Boxer. Training an older dog isn't the nightmare many adoptive owners fear. True, a puppy is a clean slate, but the older dog has probably had some training, giving you a foundation on which to build. Your adult Boxer may have unwanted behaviors to unlearn, but with time and patience, you can teach him what to do instead. An older dog also has a greater attention span and memory than a puppy and is ready and willing to do what it takes to fit in with his new pack. Positive reinforcement knows no age limits.

though, start the lesson over. He may not get this one right away, but persevere. Keep lessons short and always end in a sit, a treat, and praise.

Down

This command requires your dog to lie on his belly and stay there, which is a vulnerable position to him at first.

How to Teach Down

To teach *down*, put your Boxer in a *sit*, holding the leash in your left hand and a treat in your right. Rest a hand lightly on his shoulders. Move your treat hand in front of his nose and say, "Down," slowly lowering the treat to the floor in front of him. He will follow the path of the treat until he has lowered himself to the floor. When he reaches the ground, give him the treat and praise. Keep your movements slow and your voice soothing to ease any insecure feelings. Once he is capably performing the command, take the treat out of the equation. Eventually, he will understand what a downward hand movement and the verbal command mean.

Tricks

There are many fun ways to showcase your Boxer's talents. After he has mastered the Basic Five obedience commands, teaching him tricks can be entertaining and intellectually stimulating.

Shake Hands

This is one of the easiest tricks to teach. Start by having your Boxer sit. Say, "Shake," and take his paw in your hand. Hold it there and praise him, and then let go. Practice this several times a day. After a while, say, "Shake," but don't take his paw; see if he raises it by himself. If not, show him again by taking his paw in your hand when you give the command. He'll catch on!

Which Hand?

This old game of guessing which hand has the object is not new, but dogs clearly have the advantage here: their sensitive noses! It is not surprising that your Boxer will sniff out which of your fists conceals a treat; the trick is to get him to use his paw to indicate the correct fist. To do this, put a treat in one hand, show your Boxer, and then close both fists. Hold them in front of you about 6 inches (15.2 cm) apart and say, "Which one?" Your dog will probably pry at your fists with his mouth, but don't open them until he uses his paw (which he will, if you are patient). When he touches the correct fist with his paw, give him the treat and lots of praise.

Kiss

This one seems hardly worth teaching; Boxers have it down pat! But if you want to show off by having him give you a kiss on command, teach him to identify the word with the action. Say, "Kiss" while you offer your cheek, and praise him when he does it. If your Boxer isn't much of a licker—which is a contradiction in terms—dab a little peanut butter on your cheek, and give the command. Praise him when he licks it off. Repeat without the peanut butter.

A well-trained Boxer is a happy Boxer with a happy owner. Training gives a Boxer a "job" that this working breed needs for fulfilling its original purpose. Your payoff is in the love and loyalty your dog will give you in exchange for your efforts.

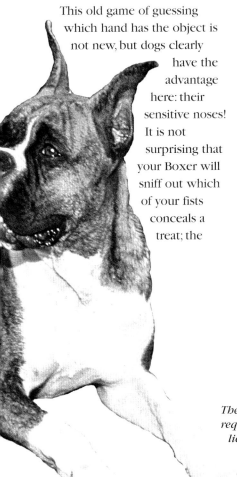

The down command requires your dog to lie on his belly and stay there.

85

Chapter 7

In the Doghouse

Even the best-behaved dogs have their moments. No matter how well trained your Boxer is, there will be a time when he doesn't do the right thing. Learning to recognize potentially habitual, unwanted behaviors is your first step toward correcting them for good.

Barking

Your Boxer's bark vocalizes any moods. A happy-sounding bark while in the play-bow means that he's having fun.

A high-pitched, yelping kind of bark might mean he's wary of something. A low, growly bark can be heard during certain kinds of play, but in other situations, it probably means "watch out!"

Barking isn't a punishable offense. It can be a good thing, especially if unwelcome strangers are around. Trouble is, the Boxer can't differentiate appropriate barking from inappropriate. He won't understand why he's a good dog for barking at a stranger but a bad

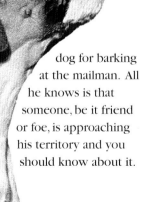

dog for barking at the mailman. All he knows is that someone, be it friend or foe, is approaching his territory and you should know about it.

Your Boxer's bark vocalizes his moods.

Solution

If barking becomes excessive and habitual, you have a problem on your hands. Behavior modification is needed, and the sooner the better.

A Boxer left alone every day for long stretches may discover that barking brings attention, even if the attention is just a neighbor yelling at him to quiet down. When you are at home together, encourage your Boxer to be quiet. If he starts barking for no reason, tell him, "Quiet!" and reward him when he stops. When he has mastered this command, leave the house for a short walk outside by yourself. Make comings and goings low profile to prevent barking from excitement. If he barks, calm him down with another "quiet!" and a treat. Take the modification a step further by talking with a neighbor outside. If your social butterfly Boxer barks in protest at being left out, correct him. Repeat these steps as necessary until he learns when not to bark.

Chewing

Chewing is mostly a problem with teething puppies. They can and will chew anything they can get their paws on, so you need to make inaccessible anything that you value or that can hurt the puppy, such as electric cords.

Solution

The best way to prevent unwanted chewing is to provide lots of safe chew

Finding the Lost Dog

Nothing is more tragic than a beloved family dog who is lost. Outfitting your Boxer with a collar and tags containing contact information provides some assurance that whoever finds him can call you. Even better are microchipping and tattooing, which cannot be removed or altered.

If your Boxer becomes lost, here's what you can do:

- Walk the neighborhood, talk to everyone, and leave your phone number in case someone spots your dog.
- The high-pitched sound of a dog whistle can carry up to a mile (1.6 km) or more. Get one and use it while you search.
- Put a strong-scented piece of clothing on your lawn or driveway. The smell can be detected from far away, and your sweaty gym socks may be the beacon that guides your dog home.
- Call local veterinary offices to ask if anyone has brought in an unfamiliar dog. Also, check with all area shelters and animal control agencies.
- Post flyers everywhere within a mile or so from the dog's last known location. Omit your name and address so that scam artists can't take advantage of you. Offer a reward, without specifying the amount. Withhold descriptions of a few unique identifying marks of your dog to use if someone says they have your pet.
- Never search for your dog alone.
- If your Boxer is microchipped or tattooed, notify the registration company that he is lost and hope that someone will find and scan him.

toys to keep your Boxer occupied. Adult dogs also enjoy chewing, and the correct chew toys help maintain healthy teeth and gums. There are scads of safe, tasty chew toys on the market with different flavors, textures, and sizes to appeal to even the most discriminating Boxer. Make sure that you select one that doesn't splinter, break, or tear, possibly causing internal injuries if consumed.

If your Boxer persists in thinking that furniture legs make the perfect chew toy, you may need to confine him to a chew-proofed area in the house. Never underestimate the Boxer's stubborn streak, though. Boxers have been known to chew the doorjamb of the room in which they are confined. The reliable crate is the safest way to protect both your Boxer and your personal effects.

Digging

Viewed by humans as a destructive behavior, digging comes very naturally

Finding a Behaviorist

The field of pet behavior is a welcome addition to the world of pet care professionals. The demand for it says that today's pet owners prefer to get rid of the unwanted behavior instead of the dog.

When researching potential behaviorists, ask about feedback from other clients, and talk to them personally if possible. When you are comfortable with the information you have garnered, phone the behaviorist for specifics on treatment principles and protocols. A qualified, conscientious professional will, in turn, ask you about your Boxer's health history, history of the current problem, and what steps have been taken already.

Sometimes our concern for our Boxers eclipses important questions about cost, equipment, length of treatment, etc. Compile a checklist to ask a potential consultant so that you will have all the information up front:

- How long will appointments be? 60 to 90 minutes is usual.

- Who must attend? Make sure all family members involved can attend.

- What will be done during these appointments? Sitting and talking? Training the dog? Different trainers have different methods and procedures, but you should know ahead of time what to expect.

- How many appointments will be required? Six weekly meetings are usual.

- What special equipment, if any, will be used? Find out exactly what the consultant plans to utilize, like spike collars, ultrasonic devices, etc. Ask for details on their purpose and usage. Do not agree to any procedure with which you are uncomfortable.

- What is the most severe physical treatment that may be required? Even if no special equipment is used, you will want to know if the consultant plans to treat your dog with kneeing, hitting, jerking, shaking, kicking, or ear biting, methods that are not only downright unacceptable but can qualify as animal cruelty. The only good answer to the question of severe physical treatment during training is "none."

- What happens if the problem persists after completion of treatment? Ask if there is a charge for post-treatment meetings.

- How much will the treatment cost? Ask what the total cost will include.

"Smooth operators" exist in every aspect of daily life, and pet care is no exception. Beware of glib consultants who try to guilt you into treatment, tell you that you will be seeing an "assistant," assure you that the program will be easy, or says you don't need to participate in the actual treatment. Give the same consideration to finding a qualified behaviorist to entrust with your Boxer's well-being as you would your own.

to dogs. Domesticated dogs are free of the burden of finding food and shelter, but not the instinct to do so. All that unchanneled energy can result in holes throughout the yard and flowerbeds. And it's not just instinct; dirt and soil are endless sources of tempting smells that Boxers can't resist. Dogs will also dig out of boredom, kind of like the couch potato who downs an entire bag of chips while watching TV.

Solution

Digging is a tricky behavior to correct, because it is hard to catch the dog in the act. By the time you notice the holes, it is too late to chastise, because your Boxer won't connect your reprimand with something he did hours earlier.

It may be easier to work with the problem than to fight it. Create a digging space especially for your Boxer. Fence off a section of your yard and allow him to dig there to his heart's content. When you are able to closely supervise him, let him have free rein in the whole yard. If he starts to dig in the wrong place, use your voice to interrupt him. Redirect him to his space, and above all, don't let him see you plant those daffodil bulbs!

Housesoiling

There is no mystery to puppy accidents. Either you relaxed supervision or you overestimated your Boxer's bladder and bowel maturity. But what if your adult Boxer starts soiling the house?

91

To combat inappropriate digging, create a specific digging space in your yard especially for your Boxer.

SENIOR DOG TIP

Training the Older Boxer With a Problem Behavior

Adopting a homeless or rescued Boxer is a loving action, but is it fair to the dog? A large household with youngsters may be just too chaotic for a traumatized Boxer, no matter how honorable your intentions. If the adult Boxer you have reared since puppyhood begins exhibiting problem behaviors, consult your vet. It is a very rare Boxer who can't be rehabilitated with the right help.

First, you need to determine the reason by making assessments based on the process of—ahem—elimination. Could it be physical? If your Boxer has been urinating more frequently and drinking more water, a urinary tract infection may be to blame. Collect a urine specimen and take it to the vet for analysis.

Solution

If nothing is physically wrong with your Boxer, consider when the soiling occurs. If it happens only when you leave the house, it could be separation anxiety. It is difficult to pinpoint why this problem pops up in adulthood, but there are several ways you can try to control it:

- Reintroduce the crate. A Boxer who soils when left alone may feel insecure for some reason, even if he never exhibited the behavior before. Even if you have previously given your adult Boxer free run of the house with no problem, you may need to reacquaint him with the security of his crate. If he soils the crate, at least your carpet will be spared while you further investigate the problem.
- Make sure that he eliminates before you leave the house, even if he already did so within the past hour. It may require a brief leash walk where scents entice him to eliminate, but it is worth making sure that he doesn't urgently *need* to eliminate while you're away.
- Don't make a big deal of your departure. Too much drama, and he'll think there's something to be anxious about! Stuff a chew toy with some peanut butter to keep him occupied. Put the radio on to keep him company, give him his treat and a "see you soon," and be on your way.
- Make sure previous accidents on carpet have been thoroughly cleaned up and odors neutralized

so that he isn't inspired to eliminate there again.

- Females over four years old are middle-aged matrons who commonly have age-related incontinence. Some urine leakage is typical, especially when the Boxer is relaxed or asleep, but large quantities of urine are not, nor is inappropriate defecation. The vet may prescribe medication to help with leaking, but be sure to address anything worse.
- If you've tried everything you can think of and your Boxer is still soiling for no apparent reason, consider consulting a behavioral specialist. You may also try prescription tranquilizers if your vet thinks they are appropriate.

In extreme cases of incontinence, doggy diapers may be the best recourse. In most cases, though, housesoiling can be managed with patience and perseverance.

Jumping Up

Boxers love people and jumping and frequently do both at once. Visitors to a Boxer's home never have to wonder where they stand! It's one thing for a puppy to jump up in greeting, but a 60-pound (27.2 kg) adult Boxer can bowl over even die-hard dog lovers who know what to expect. And let's face it: hosiery and delicate fabrics are not Boxer-resistant.

Solution

Unwanted jumping can be prevented with early training of the *sit* command. When you enter the house, resist the urge to greet your cuddly Boxer pup until you have a leash and collar in hand. Slip the collar on and tell him to sit. If he jumps up in excitement, say, "No" firmly, and put him back in a *sit.* Avoid saying, "Down" so that you don't confuse him with the command to

Unwanted jumping can be prevented with early training of the sit *command.*

FAMILY-FRIENDLY TIP

Children and Dogs With Problem Behaviors

Boxers have a natural instinct regarding children, knowing when to be extra gentle and with whom. If your Boxer is exhibiting inappropriate behavior, explain to the older children that the family as a whole must help correct it by refraining from the following:
• wild and loud behavior in the house
• emotional departures and returns
• grabbing the Boxer in a hug (perceived by the dog as a stranglehold)
• sudden movements directed at the Boxer
• interfering with mealtime or taking away a chew toy
Give both child and Boxer positive reinforcement when they behave correctly toward one another. Scrupulously supervise interaction with very young children until the problem behavior is resolved.

Another way to correct unwanted jumping is to stop it before it starts. If you think that your Boxer is about to jump on you, just walk away.

Get in the habit of putting your Boxer into a *sit* before he does anything pleasurable, including eating a meal, going for a walk, or playing fetch. You are essentially teaching him how to say "please" before indulging. He will learn that if he sits for an approaching visitor, praise and attention will follow. Enlist the help of visitors by asking them to refrain from petting your dog until he sits so that he isn't "rewarded" for incorrect behavior. In public, explain to anyone who asks to pet him to wait until the dog sits, as you're trying to teach him good manners. Even one instance of petting after jumping on someone can hamper your Boxer's progress if he decides the possibility of attention is worth the risk of displaying an incorrect behavior.

Nipping

To puppies, nipping is nothing more than a fun game. They do it with their littermates as a form of play, but when they do it to their humans, the fun stops. Our noses and ears may be great to gnaw on, but those needle-sharp puppy teeth hurt! More importantly, puppies who nip their humans are treating them as pack equals. They must learn that they are beneath you on the totem pole so that they don't grow up to be potential biters.

lie down. When he obeys, give him a treat, teaching him that good things come his way only after assuming the *sit* position.

Solution

This is a good opportunity to involve children in your Boxer's training. Explain to them that running and jumping around in the house excites the puppy, which in turn encourages him to play roughly and nip. Have the kids play outside or in another room that can be closed off until the puppy is past the teething stage. A very young child can participate by sitting on a parent's lap and offering the puppy a treat when he stops nipping at the parent's command. The goal here is to teach your child and the puppy to respect one another.

Another popular trick to cure your Boxer of nipping is the "yelp and shun" method. When the pup nips you, give a high-pitched "yelp." As soon as he lets go of your arm, hand, or whatever, turn away from him and refuse to play. This is what his littermates do when he gets too rough with

them. He will soon realize that nipping his humans causes them to turn away, and there's nothing a Boxer hates more than indifferent humans.

Redirect nipping behavior by replacing your arm with an appropriate chew toy, giving him plenty of praise when he mouths it. You can make a stronger statement with the "instant muzzle." When the puppy nips your hand, flip it to wrap around his muzzle, and hold his mouth closed for a few seconds. It won't hurt him, but he won't like it and should get the message quickly.

Boxers love people and want nothing more than to please them. With minimal training, your Boxer will be a polite, entertaining companion who will put a smile on your face for many years to come.

Safe, age-appropriate chew toys may prevent your Boxer puppy from nipping.

Chapter 8

Stepping Out

If you own a Boxer, you already know that family
outings should include all family members, both
human and canine. Dogs are social animals,
and Boxers are particularly so, craving the
companionship of their humans.

Travel and Vacationing

Once upon a time, families used to hop into their sedans and take off, blissfully ignorant about such things as air bags and seat belts.

But we know better now, and we need to enable our pets to travel with us just as safely.

Types of Travel

Your Boxer will sometimes need to travel, starting with his trip home with you, across town or across the country. Show dogs often travel far and wide on the show circuit, and many dog owners vacation only where their dog is also welcome. Every mode of transportation has its own safety concerns. Whether by road or air, safe travel with your Boxer can be a walk in the park (pun intended).

Car Travel

Your Boxer's security in the car is as important as any passenger's security. A responsible owner makes certain that her Boxer is comfortably restrained with a dog safety harness or crated. Aside from the obvious safety benefits in case of an accident, restraints prevent your Boxer from suddenly jumping up or otherwise disrupting your control of the vehicle. Car seat harnesses give your Boxer a safe and comfortable ride, as well as give you the freedom to focus on driving.

Happily crate-trained dogs can sit

Travel Essentials

You have already prepared a crate or safety harness for your motor trip, of course, but also remember to take these essentials for your traveling pooch:

- extra leash and collar with duplicate ID tags
- favorite blanket or dog bed to throw into the crate or seat for extra comfort
- some chew toys to keep him occupied during vacation down time
- first-aid kit with disinfectant, gauze pads or cotton balls, antinausea medication, tweezers for tick removal, antihistamine for insect stings, self-adhesive roll bandage
- important documentation: identification registry phone numbers, health certificates, local veterinary information
- sufficient food and water for the trip and destination
- towels to clean dirty paws, etc.
- waste removal bags—a must, no matter where you travel

This comprehensive list may seem like overkill, but if the unexpected happens, you'll be glad you're prepared.

Your dog's security in the car is as important as any human passenger's security.

back, relax, and enjoy the car ride in their crate's familiar environment, and you won't have to worry that a sudden stop will send your Boxer flying. Make sure that the crate is firmly strapped into place inside the vehicle. You don't want Boxer *and* crate to go flying in a sudden stop or fender bender, possibly causing further injury.

Never allow a dog to ride unrestrained in an open truck bed. Not only is it illegal in some areas, but it is also foolishly risky. An abrupt stop can send him tumbling around the truck bed or out into traffic. He may also see something irresistible and jump out, even if the truck is moving. And let's not even *think* what would happen in a collision.

There are two unshakeable rules for car travel. *Never* let your Boxer hold his head out of a moving car's open window. Flying debris can cause serious injury to eyes and ears. The second rule is that you should *never* leave your Boxer in a parked car, even with the windows open. A parked car heats up like a greenhouse and can rapidly cause heatstroke, a particular bane of the short-nosed Boxer. Even if the outside temperature is mild and pleasant, the car interior can heat up to a dangerous level, and open windows don't ventilate sufficiently. To spare your Boxer from a miserable death, don't leave him in a parked car. Better he stays home and misses an outing with you than risks heatstroke while you're grocery shopping.

Air Travel

Air travel can be stressful for dogs, even seasoned travelers. Historically,

Boxers and Car Phobia

Sometimes a dog requires conditioning to car travel, especially if a car ride was the first strange thing that took him away from his mother. He may also associate car trips with that person in the white coat who sticks needles into him.

Show your Boxer that cars are good and can take him to fun places. Lift a car-phobic Boxer into the parked car and give a treat, taking him out when he has finished eating it. When he is comfortable in the parked car, take him on a short ride. In a few weeks, he should be cured of any car fears

veterinarians prescribed sedatives for traveling dogs, but some experts believe that the decreased heart and respiration rates caused by sedation are more dangerous than the emotional stresses of flying. If your Boxer must travel by air, discuss sedation with your vet to decide what is best for the dog.

It is possible that the airplane can be your Boxer's only travel option, as dogs (with the exception of assistance dogs) are not permitted on commercial trains or buses, and driving can be limiting for long distances. If you plan to fly your Boxer, thoroughly research the airline's policies on dog transport, required documentation (health certificates and identification), and international quarantine laws, if applicable.

Foreign Travel

Other cultures don't always have the same regard for dogs that Americans do. Laws and restrictions regarding companion animals vary from country to country, or even within a country. Hawaii, for example, is completely rabies-free and wants to stay that way, requiring dogs relocating there from another state to be quarantined for up to 120 days.

If you are planning overseas travel for your dog, contact the local consulate for information on quarantine and health certification requirements. Check with the airlines on their regulations, and find the quickest, most direct route for your Boxer. Will a change of plane or change of airline be required? Where will the dog be during layovers? Will you have access to him? Will he be given water? Don't be shy about pressing for details. There is no such thing as a dumb question when it comes to your Boxer's safety.

Accommodations

Pet-friendly lodgings are springing up everywhere, attesting to the love people have for their pets. Hotels that welcome dogs often require a small deposit against any damage by your

FAMILY-FRIENDLY TIP

Boxer and Child: Travel Tips

Traveling with both your Boxer and your child may sound like a nightmare, but with these tips, it can be a dream:

- Stick to the child and the dog's sleeping and feeding schedules as much as possible to avoid crankiness and stress.
- Don't introduce exotic foods to Boxer or child on your trip. The diarrhea and/or nausea later will make you wish you hadn't.
- Try to find pet/child-friendly places to eat along the way. Weather permitting, a sidewalk café will let your Boxer stay near you while everyone eats.
- Pack plenty of snacks and treats, and don't be surprised if your child prefers the dog's. Healthful dog treats won't hurt your child.
- Limit sightseeing to what kids and dogs can comfortably handle. In warm weather, your Boxer can overheat quickly and tire before his humans do.
- Acknowledge your limitations with kids and dogs along. Save the museums and grand restaurants for another time, and plan a couple of afternoons at a beach, playground, or park where child and dog can stretch their legs and play for a while.
- Be mindful of other travelers who may not consider dogs or kids as cute and wonderful as you do. Keep noise down to a dull roar, and put the kibosh on unsolicited socializing.

101

Stepping Out

dog. Sometimes it is nonrefundable and used to deodorize and thoroughly clean the lodging for the next guests and their pets. Play by the rules and don't sneak your dog (although it's pretty hard to sneak a Boxer anywhere) into a lodging with a no-pets policy. If the housekeeping staff isn't aware that the room needs special cleaning, a future guest with an allergy could suffer. You should never leave your Boxer in the car all night while you sleep in the hotel. It will either be too cold or too hot, and there is always the risk of theft.

Make time in advance to search out pet-friendly accommodations along your driving route, and don't forget to stop every few hours for a leash walk and drink of water.

Taking your Boxer on vacation with you is a great way to socialize him.

102

Travel Precautions

Taking your Boxer on vacation with you is enjoyable for everyone and a great means of socialization, unless the unexpected happens. It is wise to keep an emergency kit on hand in case of illness, injury, or loss. Keep the kit updated and ready to go whenever you are. Contents should include:

- Copies of veterinary information, like your Boxer's most recent vaccination records, the name and dosage of any medications, and your vet's contact information. Search the Internet for an emergency veterinary clinic or animal hospital near your vacation spot.

- Copies of a recent photo of your Boxer to distribute if he gets lost. If he's microchipped or tattooed, be sure to bring along the registry phone numbers to report the loss. Of course, your Boxer will *always* have on a collar and leash, so the likelihood of loss is small, but better safe than sorry.

- Sufficient food and treats for the trip and a bottle of water from home. (Even slight changes in drinking water have been known to upset dogs' stomachs.) Feed your Boxer lightly on the day of departure in case of motion sickness in the car.

- Chew toys.

- Poop-scooping bags.

The golden rule of dog travel is to encourage pet-friendly lodgings to stay that way by leaving the place cleaner than you found it.

Sports and Organized Activities

The athletic, energetic Boxer is well suited to organized activities that provide a constructive outlet for all that *joie de vivre*. There is a sport for just about every taste; the hard part may be in deciding which one to pursue.

Showing Your Boxer (Conformation)

Working dogs like Boxers thrive on "jobs" where they can shine, as in the show ring. What better way to display the mutually trusting, respectful relationship you two have built?

The good-natured Boxer's intelligence—not to mention his handsome looks—makes him a natural for the show ring. As the name implies, conformation shows are competitions where entrants are evaluated against the published breed standard. Title-winning Boxers at local and regional levels go on to compete nationally against the best of the best.

To learn if your Boxer puppy has the right stuff, attend a few local shows with him and talk to other owners and handlers. Dog-training facilities often hold conformation classes to teach the basics of showing.

SENIOR DOG TIP

Traveling With the Older Boxer

The spirit is definitely still willing, but the aging Boxer may have some physical limitations to accommodate when traveling. Consider the following tips:

- Give an arthritic Boxer a leg up into the car or SUV with a ramp.
- Joint stiffness can make car rides uncomfortable. Cushion your Boxer with a memory-foam or magnet (the magnetic layer encourages circulation and eases pain) bed.
- Traveling to/through an extreme climate? Older Boxers need protection from inclement weather, so you may want to invest in some protective outerwear.

103

Stepping Out

Obedience

In dog obedience, you and your dog can compete as a team, or he can go it alone. For example, the Canine Good Citizen (CGC) trials prohibit dog owners from participating beyond verbal encouragement and praise from the sidelines. The sport of flyball, on the other hand, comprises

Pet-Friendly Lodging

teams of dogs and their humans. Unlike conformation, where appearance is everything, obedience trials showcase the handler's training ability and the Boxer's willingness to perform on command. A good starting title is the Canine Good Citizen (CGC) certificate, an AKC-sponsored award that is usually the foundation for training therapy dogs and obedience champions.

Agility

Physically demanding agility trials require dogs to navigate an intricate obstacle course within a limited time. The Boxer is swift and coordinated, but he is no match for herding breeds whose very purpose is a study in speed and agility. Nevertheless, Boxers are worthy competitors who will give it their all and have a great time doing it.

Flyball

Boxers are natural jumpers and love playing with balls. Combine the two and you have the perfect Boxer sport: flyball. Relay teams of four dogs and their owners compete simultaneously against other teams. Dogs run down a course, jumping hurdles and triggering a mechanism that spits out a tennis ball. The dog catches the ball and reverses course, and then it's the next dog's turn. The first team to have all four dogs finish wins.

Therapy Work

It has been scientifically proven that petting a dog can lower blood pressure and reduce stress. The Boxer's natural love of people makes him a perfect choice for the role of therapy dog. Patients in hospitals and nursing homes visited by therapy dogs experience raised spirits and speedier healing. A well-trained, well-socialized Boxer going into therapy work usually must complete an in-house training program for the organization providing therapy services, sometimes in addition to the

Canine Good Citizen certification. This is a goal you can both feel good about achieving.

Fun and Games

Organized sports aren't the only way to have fun with your Boxer, who would be happy to join you in almost any game you want. All you need is a little creativity. Go play!

Flying Disk

Why play flying disk with anyone else when Boxers are such great jumpers? flying disk has become a semiorganized dog sport, with tournaments and clubs. Make sure that your Boxer is in good health before engaging in any lively sport like flying disk. It's no fun if you hurt yourself or your Boxer doing it.

Balloons

An inexpensive rainy-day indoor game, a balloon is just one more thing Boxers can jump after, batting it into the air with their noses. Outside in a light breeze, it's even more fun. Keep the game confined so that your dog can't follow the balloon into an unsafe area or your neighbor's tulip bed. Retrieve any pieces of popped balloon before your Boxer has the chance to eat them.

Dogs are not so different from humans, in that insufficient fun and exercise can lead to depression, lethargy, and poor fitness. You don't have to become flyball grand champions; brisk walking or jogging every day works just as well. Your Boxer won't care much what activity he's doing, as long as he's doing it with you.

Obedience trials showcase the handler's training ability and the Boxer's willingness to perform on command.

Resources

Associations and Organizations

Breed Clubs

American Kennel Club (AKC)
5580 Centerview Drive
Raleigh, NC 27606
Telephone: (919) 233-9767
Fax: (919) 233-3627
E-mail: info@akc.org
www.akc.org

Canadian Kennel Club (CKC)
89 Skyway Avenue, Suite 100
Etobicoke, Ontario M9W 6R4
Telephone: (416) 675-5511
Fax: (416) 675-6506
E-mail: information@ckc.ca
www.ckc.ca

Federation Cynologique Internationale (FCI)
Secretariat General de la FCI
Place Albert 1er, 13
B – 6530 Thuin
Belqique
www.fci.be

The Kennel Club
1 Clarges Street
London
W1J 8AB
Telephone: 0870 606 6750
Fax: 0207 518 1058
www.the-kennel-club.org.uk

United Kennel Club (UKC)
100 E. Kilgore Road
Kalamazoo, MI 49002-5584
Telephone: (269) 343-9020
Fax: (269) 343-7037
E-mail: pbickell@ukcdogs.com
www.ukcdogs.com

Pet Sitters

National Association of Professional Pet Sitters
15000 Commerce Parkway, Suite C
Mt. Laurel, New Jersey 08054
Telephone: (856) 439-0324
Fax: (856) 439-0525
E-mail: napps@ahint.com
www.petsitters.org

Pet Sitters International
201 East King Street
King, NC 27021-9161
Telephone: (336) 983-9222
Fax: (336) 983-5266
E-mail: info@petsit.com
www.petsit.com

Rescue Organizations and Animal Welfare Groups

American Humane Association (AHA)
63 Inverness Drive East
Englewood, CO 80112
Telephone: (303) 792-9900
Fax: 792-5333
www.americanhumane.org

American Society for the Prevention of Cruelty to Animals (ASPCA)
424 E. 92nd Street
New York, NY 10128-6804
Telephone: (212) 876-7700
www.aspca.org

Royal Society for the Prevention of Cruelty to Animals (RSPCA)
Telephone: 0870 3335 999
Fax: 0870 7530 284
www.rspca.org.uk

The Humane Society of the United States (HSUS)
2100 L Street, NW
Washington DC 20037
Telephone: (202) 452-1100
www.hsus.org

Sports

International Agility Link (IAL)
Global Administrator: Steve Drinkwater
E-mail:yunde@powerup.au
www.agilityclick.com

North American Flyball Association
www.flyball.org
1400 West Devon Avenue #512
Chicago, IL 6066
800-318-6312

World Canine Freestyle Organization
P.O. Box 350122
Brooklyn, NY 11235-2525
Telephone: (718) 332-8336
www.worldcaninefreestyle.org

Therapy

Delta Society
875 124th Ave NE, Suite 101
Bellevue, WA 98005
Telephone: (425) 226-7357
Fax: (425) 235-1076
E-mail: info@deltasociety.org
www.deltasociety.org

Therapy Dogs Incorporated
PO Box 5868
Cheyenne, WY 82003
Telephone: (877) 843-7364
E-mail: therdog@sisna.com
www.therapydogs.com

Therapy Dogs International (TDI)
88 Bartley Road
Flanders, NJ 07836
Telephone: (973) 252-9800
Fax: (973) 252-7171
E-mail: tdi@gti.net
www.tdi-dog.org

Training

Association of Pet Dog Trainers (APDT)
150 Executive Center Drive Box 35
Greenville, SC 29615
Telephone: (800) PET-DOGS
Fax: (864) 331-0767
E-mail: information@apdt.com
www.apdt.com

National Association of Dog Obedience Instructors (NADOI)
PMB 369
729 Grapevine Hwy.
Hurst, TX 76054-2085
www.nadoi.org

Veterinary and Health Resources

American Animal Hospital Association (AAHA)
P.O. Box 150899
Denver, CO 80215-0899
Telephone: (303) 986-2800
Fax: (303) 986-1700
E-mail: info@aahanet.org
www.aahanet.org/index.cfm

American Holistic Veterinary Medical Association (AHVMA)
2218 Old Emmorton Road
Bel Air, MD 21015
Telephone: (410) 569-0795
Fax: (410) 569-2346
E-mail: office@ahvma.org
www.ahvma.org

Resources

American Veterinary Medical Association (AVMA)
1931 North Meacham Road – Suite 100
Schaumburg, IL 60173
Telephone: (847) 925-8070
Fax: (847) 925-1329
E-mail: avmainfo@avma.org
www.avma.org

ASPCA Animal Poison Control Center
1717 South Philo Road, Suite 36
Urbana, IL 61802
Telephone: (888) 426-4435
www.aspca.org

British Veterinary Association (BVA)
7 Mansfield Street
London
W1G 9NQ
Telephone: 020 7636 6541
Fax: 020 7436 2970
E-mail: bvahq@bva.co.uk
www.bva.co.uk

Publications

Books

Anderson, Teoti. *The Super Simple Guide to Housetraining*. Neptune City: TFH Publications, 2004.

Morgan, Diane. *Good Dogkeeping*. Neptune City: TFH Publications, 2005.

Yin, Sophia, DVM. *How to Behave So Your Dog Behaves*. Neptune City: TFH Publications, 2004.

Magazines

AKC *Family Dog*
American Kennel Club
260 Madison Avenue
New York, NY 10016
Telephone: (800) 490-5675
E-mail: familydog@akc.org
www.akc.org/pubs/familydog

AKC *Gazette*
American Kennel Club
260 Madison Avenue
New York, NY 10016
Telephone: (800) 533-7323
E-mail: gazette@akc.org
www.akc.org/pubs/gazette

The Boxer Review
8840 White Oak Avenue
Northridge, CA 91325
Telephone: (818) 885-7220
E-mail: kathy@boxerreview.com
www.boxerreview.com

Dog Fancy
Subscription Department
P.O. Box 53264
Boulder, CO 80322-3264
Telephone: (800) 365-4421
E-mail: barkback@dogfancy.com
www.dogfancy.com

Dogs Monthly
Ascot House
High Street, Ascot,
Berkshire SL5 7JG
United Kingdom
Telephone: 0870 730 8433
Fax: 0870 730 8431
E-mail: admin@rtc-associates.freeserve.co.uk
www.corsini.co.uk/dogsmonthly
Note: Boldface numbers indicate illustrations; an italic *t* indicates a table.

Index

Note: Boldface numbers indicate illustrations; an italic *t* indicates a table.

Index

110

Boxers

111

Index

Dedication
For Charlotte, Paige, and Brooke.

About the Author

Cynthia P. Gallagher lives in Annapolis, Maryland, with her husband and two Boxers. Her dog writing credits include ASPCA *Animal Watch*, *Dog & Kennel*, and *Animal Fair* magazines. Her humor column, "Boxer Shorts," appears regularly in *The Boxer Review* magazine. She is also the author of two novels under the name Cynthia Polansky. Visit her website at www.cynthiapolansky.com.

Photo Credits